Intimate Relations

Intimate

Relations

EXPLORING INDIAN SEXUALITY

Sudhir Kakar

The University of Chicago Press • Chicago

Sudhir Kakar is a distinguished psychoanalyst with a private practice in New Delhi. He is also a training analyst of the Indian Psychoanalytic Society and a senior fellow of the Centre for Developing Societies. He has taught at Harvard, McGill, and the University of Vienna and now teaches annually at the University of Chicago. His several previous books include *The Inner World* and *Shamans, Mystics, and Doctors*.

HQ
18
I4
K35
1990

The University of Chicago Press, Chicago 60637
Penguin Books India, Ltd., New Delhi, India
© 1989 by the University of Chicago
All rights reserved. Published 1990
Printed in the United States of America

99 98 97 96 95 94 93 92 91 90   54321

Library of Congress Cataloging-in-Publication Data
Kakar, Sudhir.
     Intimate Relations: Exploring Indian Sexuality / Sudhir Kakar.
          p.   cm.
     Includes bibliographical references.
     ISBN 0–226–42280–1
     1. Sex customs—India.   2. Sex role—India.   I. Title.
HQ18.I4K35   1990
306.7'0954—dc20   89–20220
                                                  CIP

For
Elisabeth and Manfred,
Anita and Vikram

Also by Sudhir Kakar

Contents

Acknowledgments

This book was largely completed during the two years I was the recipient of a Nehru Fellowship. Originally intended to be a study of family relationships in India through the medium of folktales, its focus soon narrowed to the relations between the sexes, yet also simultaneously expanded to include other narratives. I am grateful to the Jawaharlal Nehru Memorial Fund for their financial support. I am also happy to acknowledge a debt to Dr. Renuka Singh for her sensitive and skillful interviews with women from Delhi slums, which form the basis of chapter five.

Parts of this book have been presented at different forums in condensed versions. Chapters two and three were originally delivered as the George De Vos Lectures at the Department of Anthropology, University of California, Berkeley. Chapter two also formed the basis of a talk at the Department of Sociology, University of Delhi. Chapter six was presented in the Social Science Seminar at the Institute of Advanced Study, Princeton, the Department of Anthropology, Princeton University, and the Department of Political Science, Cornell University. I also wish to thank my friend John Ross for his comments and suggestions. Chapter seven was presented at the Conference on Human Development, University of Chicago, the Swiss Psychoanalytic Society, Zurich, and the Second International Psychoanalytic Symposium at Delphi. It was published under the title "The Maternal-Feminine in Indian Psychoanalysis," in the *International Review of Psychoanalysis* 16 (3), 1989, and I am grateful to the Institute of Psychoanalysis in London for their pemisssion to reprint. Finally, I wish to thank Jayashree and R. Shankar at the Centre for the Study of Developing Societies for their help in the preparation of this typescript.

Intimate Relations

1

Introduction

This book is a psychological study of the relationship between the sexes in India. It is about men and women—lovers, husbands, and wives—living in those intimate states where at the same time we are exhilaratingly open and dangerously vulnerable to the other sex. It is about Indian sexual politics and its particular language of emotions. Such an inquiry cannot bypass the ways the culture believes gender relations should be organized nor can it ignore the deviations in actual behavior from cultural prescriptions. Yet the major route I have selected for my undertaking meanders through a terrain hewn out of the *fantasies* of intimacy, a landscape whose contours are shaped by the more obscure desires and fears men and women entertain in relation to each other and to the sexual moment in which they come together. What I seek to both uncover and emphasize is the *oneiros*—the "dream"—in the Indian tale of *eros* and especially the dreams of the tale's heroines, the women.

Tale, here, is not a mere figure of speech but my chosen vehicle for inquiry and its unique value for the study of Indian gender relations, as indeed for the study of any Indian cultural phenomenon, calls for some elaboration.

The spell of the story has always exercised a special potency in the oral-based Indian tradition and Indians have characteristically sought expression of central and collective meanings through narrative design. While the twentieth-century West has wrenched philosophy, history, and other human concerns out of integrated narrative structures to form the discourse of isolated social sciences, the preferred medium of instruction and transmission of psychological, metaphysical, and social thought in India continues to be the story.

Narrative has thus been prominently used as a way of thinking, as a way of reasoning about complex situations, as an inquiry into the nature of reality. As Richard Shweder remarks on his ethnographic experiences in Orissa, whenever an orthodox Hindu wishes to prove a point

1

or convey what the world is like or ought to be like, he or she is more than likely to begin his exposition with that shift in the register of voice which is a prelude to the sentence, "Let me tell you a story."[1] The belief is widespread that stories, recorded in the culture's epics and scriptures or transmitted orally in their more local versions, reflect the answers of the forefathers to the dilemmas of existence and contain the distillate of their experiences with the world. For most orthodox Hindus, tales are a perfectly adequate guide to the causal structure of reality. The myth, in its basic sense as an explanation for natural and cultural phenomena, as an organizer of experience, is verily at the heart of the matter.

Traditional Indians, then, are imbedded in narrative in a way that is difficult to imagine for their modern counterparts, both Indian and Western. The stories they hear (or see enacted in dramas and depicted in Indian movies) and the stories they tell are worked and reworked into the stories of their own lives. For stretches of time a person may be living on the intersection of several stories, his own as well as those of heroes and gods. Margaret Egnor, in her work on the Tamil family, likens these stories to disembodied spirits which can possess (sometimes literally) men and women for various lengths of time.[2] An understanding of the person in India, especially the untold tale of his fears and wishes—his fantasies—requires an understanding of the significance of his stories.

What could be the reasons for the marked Indian proclivity to use narrative forms in the construction of a coherent and integrated world? Why is the preference for the language of the concrete, of image and symbol, over more abstract and conceptual formulations, such a prominent feature of Indian thought and culture? Partly, of course, this preference is grounded in the universal tendency of people all over the world to understand complex matters presented as stories, whereas they might experience difficulty in the comprehension of general concepts. This does not imply the superiority of the conceptual over the symbolic, of the paradigmatic over the narrative modes, and of the austere satisfactions of denotation over the pleasures of connotation. Indeed, the concreteness of the story, with its metaphoric richness, is perhaps a better path into the depths of emotion and imagination, into the core of man's spirit and what Oliver Sacks has called the "melodic and scenic nature of inner life, the Proustian nature of memory and mind."[3] For it may be, as Sacks further suggests, that the final form of the brain's record of experience and action is organized iconically and is, in fact, "art", even if the preliminary forms of cerebral representation are computational and programmatic.[4]

Apart from any possible universal grounding in brain physiology, the Indian celebration of the narrative (and the dramatic) has its roots in one of the more enduring and cherished beliefs of the culture. This particular belief holds that there is another, higher level of reality beyond the shared, verifiable, empirical reality of our world, our bodies, and our emotions. A fundamental value of most schools of Hinduism and Buddhism, the belief in the existence of an "ultimate" reality—related to ordinary, everyday reality in the same way as everyday reality is related to the dream—is an unquestioned verity of Hindu culture, the common thread in the teachings of the culture's innumerable gurus, *swamis*, and other mystics. This ultimate reality, whose apprehension is considered to be the highest goal and meaning of human life, is said to be beyond conceptual thought and indeed beyond mind. Intellectual thought, naturalistic sciences, and other passions of the mind seeking to grasp the nature of the empirical world thus have a relatively lower status in the culture as compared to meditative praxis or even art. Aesthetic and mystical experiences, as Robert Goldman has pointed out, are supposed to be closely related so that the aesthetic power of music and verse, of a well-told tale and a well-enacted play, makes them more rather than less real than life.[5] Moreover, since ultimate reality can only be apprehended experientially, its hue, flavor, and ramifications for ordinary life are best conveyed to the uninitiated mass of people in the culture through story—myth, fable, parable, and tale—thus further elevating the prestige of the narrative form. Little wonder that on occasion interrupting a story has been viewed as a sin equivalent to the killing of a Brahmin.[6]

With the declining fortunes of logical positivism in Western thought, the giving up of universalistic and ahistorical pretensions in the sciences of man and society, the traditional Indian view is not far removed from that held by some of the newer breed of social scientists. Many psychologists, for instance, believe that narrative thinking—"storying"—is not only a successful method of organizing perception, thought, memory, and action but, in its natural domain of everyday interpersonal experience, it is the most effective.[7] Other thinkers are convinced that there is no better way to gain an understanding of a society than through its stock of stories, which constitute its dramatic resources.[8] The psychoanalyst, of course, whose practice has always consisted of helping the client construct a comprehensive self-narrative that encompasses previously repressed and disavowed aspects of the self, thus making better sense of his symptoms and behavior, finds himself quite at home with the Indian insistence on story as the repository for psychological truth. At least in one influential view articulated by Ricouer, Habermas, Steele, and others, psychoanalysis is essentially telling and retelling the story of a particular life.[9] Explanation in psychoanalysis is then narrative rather than hypothetical-deductive. Its "truth" lies in the confirmatory constellation of coherence, consistency, and narrative intelligibility. Whatever else the analyst and the analysand might be doing, they are also collaborators in the creation of the story of an individual life.

The larger story of gender relations I strive to narrate here is composed of many strands that have been woven into the Indian imagination. There are tales told by the folk and the myths narrated by family elders and religious story-tellers, or enacted by actors and dancers. These have, of course, been of traditional interest for students of cultural anthropology. Today, in addition, we also have popular movies as well as modern novels and plays, which combine the society's traditional preoccupations with more contemporary promptings. I have always felt, at least for a society such as India where individualism even now stirs but faintly, that it is difficult to maintain a distinction between folktales and myths as products of collective fantasy on the one hand and movies and literature as individual creations on the other. The narration of a myth or a folktale almost invariably includes an individual variation, a personal twist by the narrator in the omission or addition of details and the placing of an accent, which makes his personal voice discernible within the collective chorus. Most Indian novels, on the other hand, are closer in spirit to the literary tradition represented by such nineteenth-century writers as Dickens, Balzac, and Stendhal, whose preoccupation with the larger social and moral implications of their characters' experiences is the salient feature of their literary creations. In other words, it is generally true of Indian literature, across the different regional languages, that the fictional characters, in their various struggles, fantasies, unusual fates, hopes, and fears, seek to represent their societies in miniature. Indeed, one of the best known Hindi novels of the post-independence era, Phanishwarnath Renu's *Maila Anchal*, goes even further in that it centers not on an individual but on a whole village. At the most, one could say that novels, films, folktales, and myths are ranged in order on a continuum which spans the expression of individual fate at one end and collective aspirations on the other. To a greater or lesser degree, the individual characters of each narrative form are symbolic revealers of a much larger universe.

In addition to drawing on the above-mentioned forms, I have also made use of other texts such as autobiography and clinical case history. In their use of imagination for the reconstruction of lives, combining facts and fictions to arrive at life-historical truth, they too are stories, strategically placed doorways into the arena of intimate relations.

My own narrative here is informed by the psychoanalytic perspective, which requires a particular kind of imagination as well as a model for interpretation. Similar to the special competence of a literary critic which enables him to "read" a poem by converting its linguistic sequences into literary structures and meanings, there is a specific kind of psychoanalytic reading—of the patient's utterances, a tale, or a myth—though, as we shall see later, not every type of narrative is read in exactly the same way. Developed through didactic analysis, clinical training, and experience, the "psychoanalytic competence" as Donald Spence has called it, consists of certain conventions that affect the analyst's overall understanding of the material and his sense of the important units of meaning.[10] To mention some of these conventions: First, there is the convention of *thematic unity*, namely, that there is an underlying commonality among separate, discrete details, whether of the therapeutic hour or of the text. Second, there is the convention of *thematic continuity*, which holds that if a patient dramatically changes the subject, or presents more than one dream during the hour, we continue to listen to the original theme through the apparent discontinuities. In other words, in spite of the narrative's postponements and detours, we keep a lookout for the recurring theme. Third, there is the convention of *thematic significance*, which holds that significant problems are always under discussion no matter how trivial the details. This convention insists that the analyst pay attention to everything while, of course, continuing to mistrust the seemingly obvious implications of what he observes. (Another convention, namely of transference, which leads an analyst to hear a patient's utterance on at least two levels—as a statement about an obvious referent and as communication about the analyst-patient relationship—applies more to the clinical situation than to the nonclinical psychoanalytic reading of texts.)

The analytic competence, the method of loosening the text, works in tandem with interpretation, as a way of reorganizing it. Whereas there is a well-defined consensus in the psychoanalytic community on "loosening," on what constitutes competence, on *how* an analyst "reads," there is no longer a similar agreement on the psychoanalytic theory that should underlie the reorganization, i.e., on *what* he has read. Although psychoanalysis has not quite fragmented into several competing frameworks, it has begun to show greater tolerance for theories other than the classical instinctual drive theory. Of course, given Freud's stature and authority within the discipline, these theories—not unlike scholarship in the Hindu tradition which permitted innovation only under the guise of interpretation—have been at pains to proclaim their fealty to the intention and concerns of the founding father. Yet the fact remains that many of these later contributions diverge in critical ways from the assumptions of drive psychology, still considered by most people outside the field as *the* "Freudian Theory."

In general, most of the newer approaches are closer to a conception of psychoanalysis as a hermeneutic enterprise concerned with reasons rather than causes, explanation rather than prediction, a *Geisteswissenschaft* of meaning and configuration rather than a natural science of mechanisms employing the metaphors of physics or chemistry. Without going into specific details, it may be noted here that the focus of these "relational" theories—to subsume the quite diverse work of theorists like Melanie Klein, Donald Winnicott, Margaret Mahler, Heinz Kohut, Erik Erikson, and Otto Kernberg, among others, under one label—is not on the derivatives of instinctual drives but on the mental representations of relationships with others which are assumed to build the fundamental building blocks of mental life.[11] There is a relative shift of emphasis in that the primary question being asked in a session changes from "What infantile wishes does this material fulfill in the patient?" to "What is the patient, as who, saying to the analyst, as whom, and from when—and why?"[12]

The theory I choose for my own work of interpretation is finally a matter of personal choice. The choice is dictated by how well the theory speaks to my own experience of the self and of others. In the last analysis, then, the criteria for selecting one theory over another are more "aesthetic" than "scientific." They have to do with my relative attraction to the *Ur*-images conjured up by different theories. On Freud's screen, there is the whirling of imperious passions, the sharp stabbings of searching, burdensome guilt. On the next screen, a post-Freudian one, there is the voracious hunger of the urge to merge and the black empty despair in absence of the other. You look into your own soul, you pay your money (in fees of the training analyst), and you take your pick. Depending upon the context, I have used both kinds of theory in my own interpretations.

Besides the analytic competence and the choice of a theoretical framework, the interpretation of a literary text also needs a model which permits the equation, in some form or other, of the literary and the psychoanalytic enterprises. In other words, in contrast to the narrative produced in the analytic situation, the psychoanalytic interpretation of other narrative forms requires, in addition, a model that allows us to regard these essentially literary and cultural narratives as if they were psychoanalytic ones.

The number of models available for our interpretative enterprise, at least as far as literary texts are concerned, is embarrassingly large. Depending upon one's attitude toward psychoanalysis and one's personal aesthetic preference for the baroque or the classical, this can denote either the richness and success of psychoanalytic theorizing or its poverty and failure to recommend the best way of going about such efforts. Traditionally, the psychoanalysis of literature has followed one or the other of these models: first, the interpretation of the unconscious motivations of fictional characters; second, the psychogenesis of the text, i.e., a psychoanalytic study of the author's life history; and third, the psychodynamics of the reader's response. To this traditional triad of character, author, and reader, Lacan has added the text. In the literary criticism influenced by him, the narrative is viewed as a movement of desire, with arousals, expectations, surprises, reversals, delays, disappointments, transformations, and fulfillments.[13] More recently, Meredith Anne Skura's influential work has suggested the reorganization of analytic models of literary interpretation into five categories: literature as case history, as fantasy, as dream, as transference, and as psychoanalytic process.[14]

In my own analysis of the more literary texts, such as the novels, I have approached them as the raw material of family case histories. Here, in the flow of events and the flux of feeling, I try to draw out some of their characters' secrets which, psychoanalysts like to believe, the authors only half knew they knew. Indeed, what makes the man-woman relationship particularly fruitful for psychoanalytic inquiry is the fact, as Freud recognized long ago, that there is nothing about which our consciousness can be so incomplete or false as about the degrees of affection or dislike which we feel for another human being. If such an attempt involves approaching the fictional characters as if they were real men and women, we should not feel discomfitted. As Joyce Carol Oates observes,

> A serious author deals only with "real" experiences and "real" emotions, though they are usually assigned to people with fictional names. I cannot believe, frankly, that anyone could—or would want to—write about experiences the

emotional equivalents of which he has not experienced personally. Writing is a far more conscious form of dreaming, and no one dreams dreams that are of no interest to him, however trivial and absurd they may appear to someone else.[15]

The narratives forming chapters of this book to which I have listened with the analyst's "third ear," possess a diversity matching that of the culture from which they originate and which, in its beliefs and attitudes toward gender relations, they seek to reflect. Modern fiction from North India, folk narratives, box office movie hits of the last twenty years, middle-aged women from the slums of Delhi recounting their lives and loves, Gandhi's autobiographical writings, case histories from the consulting rooms of Indian psychoanalysts, all have combined in the construction of the story of Indian love relations. The story is complex, played out in the cultural-psychological space that lies between universally shared wishes of the inner world and the specific restrictions placed on them by a particular society. The story's characters and the twists and turns of its plot are at times surprisingly familiar and at others utterly strange. But, then, each human culture is perhaps a kind of magical mirror for the others. Sometimes it appears to be an ordinary piece of glass coated with silver at the back which faithfully reflects the contours, planes, and details of our own familiar faces. At others, it throws up dark menacing visages, forceful intimations of our disavowed selves which we thought no longer existed. Through such a looking glass, crafted in India, let me tell a story.

2

Scenes from Marriages

Ek Chadar Maili Si (*A Sheet, Somewhat Soiled*) by the Urdu writer
Rajinder Singh Bedi, which has also recently been made into a film,
narrates the story of a poor Sikh family in a village somewhere on the
northern border of Punjab.[1] Rano, the heroine of the book, is a spirited
young woman in her early thirties. Her husband Tiloka earns a meager
living plying his *tonga* (horse carriage) for pilgrims who pass through
the village on their way to the Vaishno Devi temple in the nearby hills.
The couple has a daughter, just entering puberty, and two young sons.
The rest of the family consists of Tiloka's old parents and his twenty-
year-old younger brother Mangla.

Tiloka is a layabout and a drunkard and Rano's struggle to ensure
that he does not drink away the little money he earns is unremitting.
Rano's attempts to prevent Tiloka from drinking whenever and wherever he chooses are perceived by him as an affront to his virility, a
challenge to his overlordship as a male. The resulting quarrels are bitter
and invariably end in physical violence. In these fights Rano, using her
nails and teeth, tries to give as good as she gets, but Tiloka's superior
strength ensures that she ends up bruised and battered.

One day, Tiloka abducts a young girl pilgrim and takes her to a shady
hotel where she is raped by some of his disreputable friends. In a
macabre revenge, the girl's temporarily crazed brother kills Tiloka,
biting into his neck and drinking his blood. The village elders' council
decides that it would be best for the community and the bereaved family
if Mangla, who now drives the *tonga* and has otherwise taken his
brother's place, also takes over his wife. He should, in the language of
their community, "cover her with a sheet." Rano, who had brought up
Mangla as her own son, giving him her breasts to suck when at the birth
of her daughter the little boy too had insisted on being fed, is initially
averse to the idea of this marriage. However, she soon overcomes her
scruples. Although she views her turnabout as submission to the

collective wish, Rano secretly welcomes the the prospect of being the wife of someone who had often protected her against her drunken husband's onslaughts and toward whom she feels considerable tenderness.

Mangla, though, cannot bear the thought of a marriage with such a strongly incestuous coloring. As the time of ceremony draws near, he runs away in blind panic to hide in the fields. Hunted like a wild beast, he is caught and badly beaten by the village men. Half-senseless from the beating, he is dragged back to the house and compelled to cover Rano with a sheet.

Mangla now becomes quite withdrawn and barely goes through the motions of a family life. To Rano's considerable chagrin, and her friends' growing consternation, he refuses to consummate the marriage. One day, he finds an old bottle of liquor among his dead brother's personal effects. As he opens the bottle and as Rano makes her first protests in an eerie repetition of similar scenes with her former husband, she feels both fear and a fierce exhilaration. She dimly senses that in the impending violence Mangla will beat her like a husband and she will fight back like a wife, finally establishing a conjugal relationship which till now has only existed in the community's will. Afterwards, as she lies in bed, in excruciating pain from drunken blows, a repentant and tearful Mangla trying to staunch the flow of blood from a wound in her scalp received when he had flung her against a wall, Rano is filled with a deep satisfaction. In the preceding encounter, her body has ceased to be an object of avoidance. It has been man-handled, touched by Mangla as a husband. The marriage is consummated the same night and the couple begin to live together as husband and wife.

Rano's greatest worry now is the marriage of her daughter. The family's abysmal poverty makes it almost impossible to find a husband for the girl. Then one day, at the time of the annual festival of the local goddess, Rano is told of the arrival of a rich and handsome young man who has vowed that he will marry only Rano's daughter. The family is puzzled but nonetheless overjoyed at the good turn in their fortunes. When the procession of singing and dancing men passes by the house, the young suitor is conspicuous among them by the abjectness of his penitent mien and the frenzy of his devotion to the goddess. Rano recognizes in the man the killer of her husband, just recently released from prison. The procession stops in front of the house as if awaiting her decision. Rano is in a turmoil till her blind father-in-law tells her to regard the proposed marriage as the workings of fate, a play of unseen powers which rule over man's destiny and whose intent she should not even try to fathom. Rano consents to the nuptials of the daughter with the murderer of the girl's father, a version of the "wild man" of many an Indian tale, with whom the heroine has a sexual relationship.

Like the initial interview in clinical practice where the patient unconsciously presents his major conflict in a dramatized scene—produced by the characteristic way he uses the space of the therapist's office, the way he makes his entry and exit, the movements of his body, and his speech as he enters into a dialogue with the therapist—the novel's opening scene, too, dramatizes its main theme: the woman's wish to be valued by the husband as a woman and as a wife, that is, as *his* woman, and her longing for the tenderness such a valuation implies. The scene itself is quite short: It is late in the afternoon and the family's dog steps out into the street to find his favorite bitch lying dead. The dog sniffs at the carcass a couple of times and then unconcernedly ambles away. Rano has been watching the dog with a woman friend who remarks, "The race of men! They are all the same." Rano feels the tears smarting in her eyes but, controlling herself, attempts a mild jest. "But *your* dog is not like that!"

In the reader's mind, this short scene sets up psychological eddies which gradually spread out into wider and wider circles. Some of the dimensions of struggle between Rano and Tiloka are already sketched on the very first pages. Behind the husband and wife conflict we can sense the perennial one between man and woman which, incidentally, is explicit in the novel as it is in much of Indian domestic life and folklore. Thus, for instance, Margaret Egnor reports from Tamil Nadu:

> Within the household, as well as in the domain of paid labour, there was a strong spirit of rivalry between many women and their husbands. Wives would not automatically accept submission. Neither would their husbands. Consequently, their relationship was often, from what I was able to observe, disputatious . . . . The eternal conflict between spouses is abundantly reflected in Indian mythology, especially Tamil which debates the issues of male vs. female superiority back and forth endlessly on a cosmic level in the form of battles and contests between deities or demons and their real or would-be mates.[2]

In folklore, Shiva and Parvati, for instance, argue interminably as to who is the better dancer, while Vishnu and Lakshmi need to descend to earth to find out which of them is the greater divinity.

Now in most regions of the country, male folk wisdom offers similar overt reasons for man's perennial war with woman. It agrees in portraying the female sex as lacking both sexual morality and intelligence. Punjabis and Gujaratis are of one mind that "The intelligence of a woman is in her heels" (*Strini akkal edi mā*).[3] Tamils maintain that "No matter how educated a woman is, her intelligence is always of the lowest order," and Malayalis warn that "One who heeds the advice of a woman will be reduced to beggary" (*Penachollu Kalkkunnavanu peruvali*). Folk sayings in the northern languages, however, place singularly greater emphasis on the employment of force and physical chastisement to correct perceived female shortcomings. "The place of a horse and a woman is under the thighs" (*Ghoda aur aurat rān talē*) we hear in Hindi. And in Gujarati, "Barley and millet improve by addition of salt, women through a beating by a pestle" (*Usī jawār bājrī musē nār pādhrī*): "Better to keep the race of women under the heel of a shoe" (*Rāndni jāt khāsdane talē rākhelij bhalī*); (*Mūrkh nāri ne nagārā kutyani kāmnā*). The proverbs in the South Indian languages, on the other hand, convey more a man's sense of helplessness and resignation in the face of general female cussedness and constant provocation. "Wind can be held in a bag, but not the tongue of a shrew," is common to both Kannada and Telugu. "Neither the husband nor the brother-in-law can control a pugnacious woman" goes another Telugu saying, while yet another admits even a king's helplessness in the face of female disputatiousness.

Like wives in other novels, Rano uses words, biting, scornful words that seek to humble male pretensions—to enrage an already furious spouse. She taunts the husband to do his worst as far as physical battering is concerned and then emerges bloody but triumphant, victorious in that she denied him her submission to his will.

Rano's chief weapon in her battle against Tiloka, a weapon she is constantly seeking to hone and make more effective, is her attempted control over Tiloka's sexual appetites. When she goes to the village *baba* (holy man) for a charm, it is for a spell which puts her husband in her power—a charm even more coveted by the village women than the talisman for the birth of a child. The tablet which the *baba* gives is for the sexual enthrallment of the husband. If it works, Rano fantasizes, she would refuse Tiloka all sexual access. Only after a long stretch of his begging and entreaty, his throwing himself at her feet in abject submission, rubbing his nose on the ground in repentant surrender, might she just allow him to approach her in carefully rationed doses.

Rano's need for the charm is far removed in intent from similar quests by women (for instance that of Sachi, Indra's wife) mentioned in the *Rig-* and *Atharva-vedas*, in which spells are sought to win the love of the husband from other co-wives.[4] Female sexuality for Rano and her friend is very much a utilitarian affair whose chief value lies in its capacity to redress a lopsided distribution of power between the sexes.

Finding a suitable object in her husband, Rano's hostility against the "race of men" is split off from her erotic promptings. Without the tenderness of love to neutralize or transform it, her rage is rampant, unappeased even by Tiloka's murder. When she views Tiloka's corpse, Rano's first impulse is to celebrate by decking herself in all finery. She has to squeeze an onion into her eyes and remind herself of the miserable fate awaiting her as a widow before she can shed the tears expected of her. She can cry only for herself. Rano's love, both in its affectional and sensual currents, has to seek another object within the family.

Traditionally, this object has often been the husband's younger brother. For a time in Indian social history, the erotic importance of the brother-in-law—in the sense that he would or could have sexual relations with his elder brother's widow—was officially recognized in the custom of *niyoga*. The custom itself goes back to the times of the *Rig-veda* where a man, identified by the commentators as the brother-in-law, is described as extending his hand in promised marriage to a widow inclined to share her husband's funeral pyre.[5]

Though the custom gradually fell into disuse, especially with the prohibition of widow remarriage, surviving only among remote communities such as the hillsmen of Uttar Pradesh, the psychological core of *niyoga*, namely the mutual awareness of a married woman and her younger brother-in-law as potential or actual sexual partners, is very much an actuality even today. The awareness is present in the chastest of mythical wives, Sita, who, in the *Ramayana*, accuses Lakshmana of hesitating to help her husband and his brother, Rama, because of his feelings for her. As Lakshmana later reports the conversation to Rama: "Sita said to me, 'Evil one, an excess of feelings for me has entered you. But if my husband is destroyed, you will not obtain me.'"[6] Expressed in a certain tenderness, in erotically tinged banter, or cases of actual physical intimacy, the relationship is very much a part of a marriage's emotional space.[7] In clinical practice, I have found that women who are on terms of sexual intimacy with a brother-in-law rarely express any feelings of guilt. Their anxiety is occasioned more by his leaving home or his impending marriage, which the woman perceives as an end to her sensual and emotional life.

The disquieting murmurs of incestuous tensions have been the stuff of much drama and the distress of Rano and Mangla at their impending marriage are riveting for this reason alone. Mangla's suffering, however, in the face of a long-awaited denouement to the incestuous wish, the embodiment in the flesh of fantasy hitherto entertained in the imagination alone, is much greater than Rano's. He is like the boy who feels he bears the full culpability of being aroused by his mother. Beleaguered by his erotic yearnings for her, he does not truly conceive of hers for him. Rano, in contrast, is relatively more matter-of-fact and accepting of the paradoxes of the sexual realm. Perhaps like many other women, she seems better able to cope with the guilt of incestuous urgings than her "son" who must first beat her for their impending transgression before he can accept his disturbing and dangerous sensual immersion.

Krishna Sobti's *Mitro Marjani*, another novel with a similar theme, is less a story than a portrait of a woman, with a lower-middle-class family life sketched in as the background.[8] The book is dominated by its heroine, a young Punjabi woman called Mitro. Her husband, the two brothers-in-law and their wives, the husband's old parents, are all bit players in the dramatization of her desire, existing only to enhance and provide counterpoints to Mitro's moods and actions.

As in *Ek Chadar*, the beginning of the novel features a violent quarrel between the husband and wife. Sardari, Mitro's husband, is hitting her while Mitro stands still, her eyes raised to his face in defiance. "Will you lower your eyes or not?" the husband keeps asking her with each blow. A stubborn Mitro refuses to look down, denying him this token of her submission. The mother-in-law, a representative of the older generation of women, pleads with her, "If he is stubborn, why don't *you* lower your gaze, daughter? How can we helpless women confront men who are our lords?"

The running battle between husband and wife, we learn later, is not only around the theme of dominance and submission, a trial of strength over the distribution of power between the two sexes. Mitro's husband suspects her of promiscuous tendencies, a belief the spirited young woman does nothing to dispel. Indeed, she underlines this impression by the evident pride she takes in the fullness and bloom of her body, the sexual banter she carries on with her brother-in-law, and the candid confession of her sexual hunger to her sister-in-law. "Have you seen such breasts on another woman?" she asks in innocent yet deeply sensual self-satisfaction as she strips off her clothes. "Your *devar* (younger brother-in-law, i.e., Mitro's husband) does not recognize my disease. At the most he approaches me once a week or fortnight . . . this body is so thirsty that it thrashes around like a fish out of water." The sister-in-law, a good, conventional wife, is scandalized. For her, a woman's body is not an object of pride or pleasure but something that is made impure every day, an abode of sinfulness. Angrily, she counters Mitro's desires with the sanctimonious cultural definition of the woman's role in Hindu society: "For daughters and daughters-in-law the ways of her home and household are like *Lakshmana-rekha.** Knowingly or unknowingly, if this line is ever breached. . . .", the unfinished sentence leaving behind in the trailing silence a stark intimation of disaster.

Mitro, however, is frankly open in the expression of her physical needs as a woman and in the mockery of her husband's inability to satisfy them. Once, when her mother-in-law mentions the pregnancy of her elder sister-in-law and seeks to console Mitro by saying, "When you open up it won't be one but seven who will be playing around in the courtyard," Mitro retorts:

If it was in my power I would bear one hundred *kauravas*
(the 'evil' clan in the epic *Mahabharata*) but, mother, first
do something about your son to produce some movement in
that useless statue of stone.

The family, already reeling under the dishonest business dealings of the youngest son, who has left the house along with his wife, fear that Mitro's brazen behavior will soon cause further scandal. They ask her to go to her mother's home for a while. Mitro, anticipating the freedom and ample opportunity for erotic liaison available at her mother's home—the mother is widely regarded as a fallen woman for her long-standing affair with a village official—is overjoyed at the prospect. Sardari, her husband, accompanies her on the visit. Mitro narrates her predicament to her mother who offers to help her out, to "call a gardener for her garden" as she puts it. She even offers to keep a guard over her sleeping son-in-law's door and arranges for the daughter to visit her own lover. On the evening of the assignation, Mitro dresses like a dancing girl. In trying to make her husband drunk she behaves with the

* The line drawn by Lakshmana around Sita within which no harm could befall her.

15

coquetry of an expensive whore in a high-class brothel, to the inebriated Sardari's early horror and eventual delight. When the husband sinks into a drunken stupor, Mitro is ready to go to the waiting man but is stopped by the weeping mother who has had second thoughts. Mitro goes back to her husband's room. When they wake up in the morning, she embraces him tightly and covers his face with kisses, expressing her affection for the husband as intensely as she had shown desire for adulterous sex in the previous evening.

My choice of *Ek Chadar* and *Mitro Marjani* has been dictated by my feeling, based on personal and professional experience, that their portrayal of the man-woman relationship has aspects with considerable potential for generalization. As with Freud's *Rat Man*, a single case history which later proved to be psychodynamically representative for a host of other cases of obsessional-compulsive neurosis, fictional family histories too may illuminate significant themes in Indian marriages in situations quite different from their novelistic origins. That these themes relate to conflict in marriage, rather than to happiness and contentment, is of course embedded in the nature of the fictional enterprise itself. If happy families, as Tolstoy asserted, are all alike, then happy marriages have no history and consequently "They lived happily ever after" marks the end of the story rather than its beginning or middle. Of course, the abstraction of these themes from the novels in the form of generalizations must emerge through a careful engagement with other cultural-historical and social-anthropological materials dealing with marriages and the man-woman relationship in India. Fiction and what I like to call cultural psychology—the psychic representation in individuals of their community's history and social institutions—can reciprocally illuminate each other.

In her frank sexuality, and restlessness, and in her straining against the confines of a cultural role she finds too restrictive, Mitro is certainly a woman unusual for her milieu and class. Superior to the role in life in which she finds herself, struggling against a confining cultural fate, Mitro is the kind of troubled character who, all over the world, is a favorite of both novelists and healers of the soul. Like many women in India, in fiction and in life, she expresses her rage through words, or better, verbal barbs poisoned with ridicule and sharpened with the cutting edge of sarcasm. Yet even at the beginning of the story, we sense that Mitro's conflict, as she pushes against restraining cultural walls, is too deep to be bridged by a creative coining of sarcastic phrases. We fear that if she is unable to get greater space for herself, she will become violent, self-destructive, or apathetic.

To me, *Mitro Marjani* is one of the more explicit renderings of a muted yet extremely powerful theme in Hindu marriages: the cultural unease, indeed, the fear of the wife as a woman, i.e., as a sexual being. More exactly, it is the age-old yet still persisting cultural splitting of the wife into a mother and a whore which underlies the husband-wife relationship and which explains the often contradictory Hindu views of the woman. The mother-whore dichotomy is of course a well-known Freudian syndrome which describes the separation of sexuality from tenderness, the object of desire from the object of adoration. Freud has described the psychodynamics of this occurrence in which a man idealizes one kind of a woman, generally of his own social class. She is seen as "higher" and "purer" than him, but he is impotent with her, while on the other hand he is capable of sexual relations with a woman of a lower social station, very frequently a prostitute.[9] This split can often be traced back to the anxiety surrounding incestuous imaginings and, with it, a horror of "de-idealizing" a mother on whose image, in its purity, the man-boy still relies for nurturance and undying support. The splitting of the mother-image into the goddess and whore allows the man to have a modicum of sexual life without being overwhelmed by anxiety.

The mother-whore dichotomy or, in its Hindu version, the mother-whore-partner-in-ritual trichotomy, is crucial for understanding the culture's public and official attitudes toward women and wives. Manu, the Hindu law-giver, and his subsequent commentators, who have formulated the society's formal view of the other sex, have perhaps been unjustly branded as misogynists. A careful reading of their texts shows that misogyny as well as the praise of women follows a purely contextual course. In other words, a wife is not a wife in and for all seasons; it is the context which determines whether she is regarded as good, bad, or divine. As a partner to her husband in the prescribed sacrifices to ancestors and gods, that is, in the context of the ritual, the wife is a respected being. Manu can thus say, "Where women are honored, there the gods are pleased; but where they are not honored, no sacred rite yields rewards."[10] In her maternal aspect, actual or potential, a wife is again a person deserving of all reverence. "Between wives who [are destined] to bear children, who secure many blessings, who are worthy of worship and irradiate [their] dwellings and between the goddesses of fortune [who reside] in the houses [of men], there is no difference whatsover."[11] It is only just as a woman, as a female sexual being, that the patriarchal culture's horror and scorn are heaped upon the hapless wife.

It is clear from its context that the oft-quoted verse, "Her father protects her in childhood, her husband protects her in youth and her sons protect her in old age; a woman is never fit for independence,"[12] refers to a "protection" not from external danger but from the woman's inner, sexual proclivities. Thus the previous verse talks of controlling her attachment to sensual enjoyments. The subsequent one calls reprehensible the father who does not give her away in marriage at puberty; the husband who does not approach her sexually when she is in her season(*ritu*); and the son who after his father's death does not protect the mother—from the attentions of other men and from her own urges, the implication is clear.

In fact the first twenty-six stanzas of the chapter "Duties of Husband and Wife" in *The Laws of Manu*, which form the cornerstone of the culture's official view of women, can be read as a fantasy around the theme of the adult woman's possible sexual abandon and potential infidelity. The fantasy is very much that of the Oedipal boy who imagines the mother turning away from him and toward the father and his man-sized penis. She is a siren and has but seduced and abandoned him.

The fantasy thus starts with the wish to "guard" a woman from her overwhelming sexual temptation and from the interlopers who would exploit it for their own and her pleasure. Yet guarding her by force is not realistically possible, and perhaps it is better to keep her thoroughly engaged in household work and thus fancy-free. "Let the [husband] employ his [wife] in the collection and expenditure of his wealth, in keeping [everything] clean, in [the fulfillment of] religious duties, in the preparation of his food, and in looking after the household utensils."[13] On the other hand, even the dam of "busy-ness" is really not enough to constrain her erotic turbulence and our Oedipal lover appeals to her conscience, the inner sentinel. "Women confined in the house under trustworthy and obedient servants, are not (well) guarded, but those who of their own accord keep guard over themselves, are well guarded."[14] Both the recourse to the external world and to the woman's own superego do not prove to be sufficient as the more primitive images in the jealous and disappointed lover's fantasy break through to the surface. "Women do not care for beauty, nor is their attention fixed on age; [thinking], '[It is enough that] he is a man,' they give themselves to the handsome and the ugly."[15] "Through their passion for men, through their mutable temper, though their natural heartlessness, they become disloyal toward their husbands, however carefully they may be guarded in this [world]."[16] "[When creating them] Manu allotted to

18

women [a love of their] bed, [of their] seat and [of] ornament, impure desires, wrath, dishonesty, malice, and bad conduct."[17] Anger and retaliation now follow wherein the woman must atone for her lapse before she can again be resurrected as the pure and the needed mother. The mantra she needs to recite for the "expiation of her sins" is not hers but in fact that of the son: "If my mother, going astray and unfaithful, conceived illicit desires, may my father keep that seed from me."[18] Punished and repentant, the whore finally disappears, to be replaced by the untainted mother who, in subsequent verses, is praised and equated with the goddess (of fortune).

The image of the wife as the needed mother and the feared whore is even today reflected in the proverbs of all the major Indian languages, a testimony to the cultural unity of the subcontinent in the way fundamental human relationships—between spouses, siblings and generations—are viewed.[19] As one would surmise, woman's infidelity is the major theme in the various proverbs seeking to grasp the nature of the feminine. "Only when fire will cool, the moon burn or the ocean fill with tasty water will a woman be pure," is one of the many Sanskrit pronouncements on the subject. "A woman if she remains within bounds; she becomes a donkey out of them," say the Tamils. The exceptional proverbs in praise of wives, for instance in Assamese and Bengali, invariably and predictably address their maternal aspect — "Who could belittle women? Women who bear children!" A Punjabi proverb puts the husband's dilemma and its resolution in a nutshell, "A woman who shows more love for you than your mother is a slut."

It is evident that with such a collective fantasy of the wife, the fate of sexuality *within* marriage is likely to come under an evil constellation of stars. Physical love will tend to be a shame-ridden affair, a sharp stabbing of lust with little love and even less passion. Indeed, the code of sexual conduct for the householder-husband fully endorses this expectation. Stated concisely in the *smritis* (the Law codes), elaborated in the *puranas* (which are not only collections of myths but also contain chapters on the correct conduct of daily life), modified for local usage by the various kinds of *religiosi*, the thrust of the message seems to be, "No sex in marriage please, we're Indian."

Consider: A husband should only approach a woman in her season (*ritu*), a period of sixteen days within a menstrual cycle. "But among these the first four, the eleventh and thirteenth are [declared to be forbidden]; the remaining nights are recommended."[20] The availability of ten nights a month for conjugal relations is only an apparent largesse. The Hindu counterparts of Blake's priests in "black gowns, walking

19

their rounds and binding with briars my joys and desires" have not yet finished with their proscriptions. Since the all-important sons are conceived only on even nights, while daughters are conceived on uneven ones, the number of recommended nights straightaway shrinks by a half. Then there are the *parvas*, the moonless nights and those of the full moon, on which sexual relations lead either to the "hell of feces and urine" (Vishnu Purana) or to the birth of atheist sons (Brahma Purana). In addition, there are many festival days for gods and ancestors which are forbidden for any erotic transports. Thus the likelihood that most of the remaining five nights are sexually safe decreases greatly. Moreover, it is not a matter of permitted and forbidden nights (sex during the day is, of course, beyond the pale). The question is of a general disapproval of the erotic aspect of married life, a disapproval which is not a medieval relic but continues to inform contemporary attitudes. This is quite understandable since changes in sexuality occur at a more gradual pace than transformations in the political and social sphere; sexual time beats at a considerably slower pace than its chronological counterpart.

Sexual taboos, then, are still so strong among some Hindu communities that many women, especially from the higher castes, do not have a name for their genitals. At the utmost, the genitals are referred to obliquely—for instance "the place of peeing," though even this euphemism carries a strong affective charge. One patient, educated in England, did not have any trouble in mentioning her sexual parts as long as she could do so in English. If asked to translate the words into her mother tongue, the language nearer her early bodily experience, she would either "forget" the appropriate words or freeze into a long silence which all her conscious efforts could not break. Ignorance, of course, thrives in the socially generated pall of silence. One college-educated patient believed well into her late teens that menstrual blood, urine and babies all came out through the urethra. Another woman, brought up in a village and presumably more familiar with the "barnyard" facts of life, realized with deep consternation only when giving birth to her first child that babies were not born through the anus as she had believed. Writing on Indian sexuality some two thousand years after the *Kamasutra*, I still cannot say to its author — "Elementary, dear Vatsayana."

Of course, the modern notion of sexuality diverges in essential ways from that of Vatsayana, a change to which psychoanalysis has significantly contributed. Sexual need in the psychoanalytic sense is not a need for coitus, and sexuality is neither equated with genitality nor with the expression of a biological drive. The psychoanalytic concept of sexuality is far more than simple genital conjunction or a question of "fit" in organ sizes. A mental absence of satisfaction can exist where there is no lack of normal sexual intercourse. Sexuality, in psychoanalysis, is a system of conscious and unconscious human fantasies, arising from various sources, seeking satisfaction in diverse ways, and involving a range of excitations and activities that aim to achieve pleasure that goes beyond the satisfaction of any basic somatic need.

What we are talking of here is the cultural impact on *psycho*sexuality in Indian marriage. Cultural injunctions perhaps do not affect the act of coitus or regulate its transports. What they can do, though, is to increase the conflicts around sexuality, sour it for many, and generally contribute towards its impoverishment. This can effectively block many men and most women from a deep full experience of sexual love and the mutual cherishing of bodies, the only containers we have of our souls. Cultural injunctions become significant for the family since a fundamental aspect of the relationship between the parents involves the meaning of each child in terms of the parents' conscious and unconscious fantasy around the act that produced the conception. And if one agrees with Winnicott, as I do, that the way we arrange our families practically shows what our culture is like, just as a picture of the face portrays the individual, then beliefs and norms around sexuality in marriage gain a wider significance for the understanding of culture.[21]

The considerable sexual misery is not only a postulate inferred from Hindu cultural ideals and prohibitions relating to sex in marriage or deduced from interpretations of modern fiction. Even discounting the sexual woes of a vast number of middle- and upper-class women who come for psychotherapy as being an unrepresentative sample, there are other, direct indications that sexual unhappiness is also widespread in the lowest castes whom the upper sections of society have always imagined to be free of the culture's restrictive mores. Thus interviews with low-caste, "untouchable" women from a poor locality in Delhi, most of them migrants from villages of Uttar Pradesh, revealed sexuality pervaded by hostility and indifference rather than affection and tenderness. Most women portrayed even sexual intercourse as a furtive act in a cramped and crowded room, lasting barely a few minutes and with a marked absence of physical or emotional caressing. Most women found it painful or distasteful or both. It was an experience to be submitted to, often from a fear of beating. None of the women removed their clothes for the act since it is considered shameful to do so. Though some of the less embittered women still yearned for physical tenderness from the husband, the act itself was seen as a prerogative and need of the male — "*Admi bolna chahta hai* (Man wants to speak)."

If we agree with Lakoff and Johnson that human thought processes are largely metaphorical, that we understand and experience things and concepts in the network of their metaphorical affinities, then it is instructive to look at other metaphors used by this group of women for what in English is called "love-making."[22] "*Hafte mein ek bar lagwa lete hain* (I get it done to me once a week)," has in its original Hindustani the connotations of a weekly injection, painful but perhaps necessary for health. The most common expressions for intercourse are *kaam* and *dhandha*, work and business. Sexual intercourse for these women (and men) seems to be structured in terms of contractual and impersonal exchange relations, with the ever-present possibility of one party exploiting or cheating the other.

The conflict between the sexes in marriage, which I have charted out in this chapter, is not devoid of moments of tenderness between the spouses and, especially for the women, the feelings of loss and mourning at its absence. Mitro's occasional gestures of physical affection and of financial generosity toward Sardari when the family is in deep financial trouble, or Rano's deeply felt anguish and regret as she tells Mangla that the war between the sexes is like that of the *Mahabharata*, are just two illustrative scenes from our novels. Indeed, Rano's analogy of the Kurukshetra battle is an apt characterization of the basic struggle between husbands and wives. The war is between antagonists who know each other well, even have loyalty and admiration for one another member of the enemy host, and where regular pauses in the daily hostilities do take place.

What these novels only hint at and which becomes an overwhelming issue in fiction (and patients) from (and of) the middle- and upper-middle-class social milieu is the profound yearning of a wife, as a woman, for a missing intimacy with the husband—as a man. Generally fated for disappointment, the fantasy of constituting a "couple," not in opposition to the rest of the extended family but within this wider network, is a dominant theme running through women's lives, actual and fictional. Connecting the various stages of a woman's adulthood, from an expectant bride to a more sober grandmother, the intense wish to create a two-person universe with the husband where each finally "recognizes" the other, is never far from her consciousness. It stands as a beacon of hope amidst the toil, drudgery, fights, disappointments, and occasional joys of her stormy existence within the extended family. In contrast to much of popular Western fiction, the Indian "romantic" yearning is not for an exploring of the depths of erotic passion, or for being swept off the feet by a masterful man. It is a much quieter affair, with the soul of a Mukesh-song, and when unsatisfied this longing shrivels the emotional life of many women, making some go through life as mere maternal automatons. Others, though, react with an inner desperation where, as one woman put it, even the smell of the husband is a daily torture that must be borne in a silent scream. The desired intimacy, forever subduing the antagonism between husband and wife, inherent in the division of sexes and culturally exaggerated, is the real *sasural*—the husband's home—to which a girl looks forward after marriage and which even a married woman keeps on visiting and revisiting in the hidden vaults of her imagination.

3

Lovers in the Dark

When I was growing up in the 1940s, going to the cinema, at least in the Punjab and at least among the middle- and upper-classes, was regarded as slightly dissolute, if not outright immoral, and the habit was considered especially dangerous to the growing sensibilities of young children. Of course not all films were equally burdened with disapproval. Like everything else in India—from plants to human beings—there was (and is) a strict hierarchical classification. In the movie caste system, stunt films, the Indian version of Kung Fu movies, were the low-caste Shudras at the lowest rung of the ladder while the Brahmin "mythologicals" and the Kshatriya "historicals" vied for supermacy at the top. The only time I was admitted to the owner's box of Prabhat Talkies—the cinema owned by a grand-uncle in Lahore—was to see an eminently forgettable mythological called *Kadambari*. In childhood, stunt films were my favorite, although my taste was quite catholic, consisting as it did of indiscriminate adoration. With the complicity of a friendly doorman who doubled as an odd-job man in my grand-uncle's adjoining house, I was in the fortunate position of being able to indulge my secret passion for films whenever we visited Lahore. I use the word "passion" literally and not as a metaphor, since my craving for movies was insatiable and my consumption equally remarkable; I saw *Ratan* sixteen times, *Shikari* fourteen times, and even *Kadambari* three times after that first viewing from the owner's box.

I remember my movie-going with a nostalgia which cloaks childhood events, at least the good ones, in a unique glow of permanence and ephemerality. In the anonymity of a darkness pierced by the flickering light which gave birth to a magical yet familiar world on the screen, I was no longer a small boy but a part of the envied world of adulthood, although I sensed its rituals and mysteries but dimly. I always joined in the laughter that followed a risqué comment, even if its exact meaning escaped me. I too would hold my breath in the hushed silence that

25

followed a particularly well-enacted love scene, and surreptitiously try to whistle with the O of the thumb and the index finger under the tongue, in imitation of the wolf-whistles that greeted the obligatory scene in which the heroine fell into the water or was otherwise drenched. Recently, when in *Satyam Shivam Sundaram* Miss Zeenat Aman's considerable charms were revealed through her wet and clinging saree at the receiving end of a waterfall, I felt grateful to the world of Hindi movies for providing continuity in an unstable and changing world. When I was a child, the movies brought the vistas of a desirable adulthood tantalizingly close; as an adult, I find that they help to keep the road to childhood open.

I have described my engagement with the world of Hindi films at some length, not in order to claim any vast personal experience or specialized knowledge but to stress the fact of an enduring empathic connection with the world of Indian popular cinema. Today, this cinema, which draws upon images and symbols from the traditional regional cultures and combines them with more modern Western themes, is the major shaper of an emerging, pan-Indian popular culture. Though its fixed repertoire of plots, with which the audience is presumably thoroughly familiar, has striking parallels with traditional folk theater, the popular culture represented by the cinema goes beyond both classical and folk elements even while it incorporates them.

The appeal of the film is directed to an audience so diverse that it transcends social and spatial categories. Watched by almost fifteen million people every day, popular cinema's values and language have long since crossed urban boundaries to enter the folk culture of the rural-based population, where they have begun to influence Indian ideas of the good life and the ideology of social, family, and love relationships. The folk dance of a region or a particular musical form such as the devotional *bhajan*, after it has crossed the portals of a Bombay or Madras studio, is transmuted into a film dance or a film *bhajan* by the addition of musical and dance motifs from other regions as perhaps also from the West, and is then relayed back in full technicolor and stereophonic sound to decisively alter the original. Similarly, film situations, dialogue, and decor have begun to colonize folk theater. Even the traditional iconography of statues and pictures for religious worship is paying homage to film representations of gods and goddesses.[1]

My own approach to popular cinema is to think of film as a collective fantasy, a group daydream. By "collective" and "group" I do not mean that Hindi film is an expression of a mythic collective unconscious or of something called a group mind. Instead, I see the cinema as the primary vehicle for shared fantasies of a vast number of people living on the Indian subcontinent who are both culturally and psychologically linked. I do not use "fantasy" in the ordinary sense of the word, with its popular connotations of whimsy, eccentricity, or triviality, but as another name for that world of imagination which is fueled by desire and which provides us with an alternative world where we can continue our longstanding quarrel with reality. Desire and fantasy are, of course, inexorably linked. Aristotle's dictum that there can be no desire without fantasy contains even more truth in reverse. Fantasy is the *mise-en-scène* of desire, its dramatization in a visual form.

The origins of fantasy lie in the unavoidable conflict between many of our desires, formulated as demands on the environment (especially on people), and the environment's inability or unwillingness to fulfill our desires, where it does not proscribe them altogether. The power of fantasy, then, comes to our rescue by extending or withdrawing the desires beyond what is possible or reasonable, by remaking the past and inventing a future. Fantasy, the "stuff that dreams are made of," is the bridge between desire and reality, spanning the chasm between what is asked for and what is granted. It well deserves psychoanalyst Robert Stoller's paean as "the vehicle of hope, healer of trauma, protector from reality, concealer of truth, fixer of identity, restorer of tranquility, enemy of fear and sadness, cleanser of the soul."[2] Hindi films, perhaps more than the cinema of many other countries, are fantasy in this special sense.

The sheer volume of unrelieved fantasy in one film after another is indeed overwhelming, and it is disquieting to reflect that this exclusive preoccupation with magical explanations and fairy-tale solutions for life's problems could be an expression of a deep-seated need in large sections of Indian society. Some may even consider such a thorough-going denial of external reality in Indian cinema to be a sign of morbidity, especially since one cannot make the argument that fantasy in films fulfills the need for escapism of those suffering from grinding poverty. In the first place, it is not the poor who constitute the bulk of the Indian film clientele. In the second, one does not know the cinema of any other country which, even in the worst periods of economic deprivation and political uncertainty, dished out such uniformly fantastic fare. Neither German cinema during the economic crisis of the 1920s nor Japanese cinema in the aftermath of the Second World War elevated fantasy to such an overwhelming principle. And if one considers that neorealism even flourished in Italy during the economic chaos following the Allied victory, then one must acknowledge that economic conditions alone cannot explain the fantasia permeating Indian films.

The reason for the ubiquity of fantasy in the Hindi cinema, I suspect, lies in the realm of cultural psychology rather than in the domain of socio-economic conditions. Now, as in other cultures, we too have our film addicts. These are the unfortunate people who were pressed in childhood to view reality in an adult way and now need the fantasy of the film world to fill up the void left by a premature deprivation of magic in early life. Leaving aside this group, no sane Indian believes that Hindi films depict the world realistically, although I must admit I often feel that our willingness to suspend disbelief is relatively greater than in many other cultures. This is not because the thought processes of Indians are fantasy-ridden. The propensity to state received opinion and belief as observation, to look for confirmation of belief rather than be open to disturbing new knowledge, to generally think in a loose, associative rather than a rigorous and sequential way, is neither Indian, American, Chinese, Japanese, or German, but common to most human beings. However, I would hypothesize, without passing any value judgment, that, relatively speaking, in India the child's world of magic is not as far removed from adult consciousness as it may be in some other cultures. Because of a specific thrust of the culture and congruent childrearing practices which I have described in detail elsewhere, the Indian ego is flexible enough to regress temporarily to childhood modes without feeling threatened or engulfed.[3] Hindi films seem to provide this regressive haven for a vast number of our people.

If, as I have indicated above, I regard the Indian cinema audience not only as the reader but also as the real author of the text of Hindi films, what is the role played by their ostensible creators—the producers, directors, scriptwriters, music directors, and so on? In my view, their functions are purely instrumental and akin to that of a publisher who chooses, edits, and publishes a particular text from a number of submitted manuscripts. The quest for the comforting sound of busy cash registers at the box office ensures that the filmmakers select and develop a daydream which is not idiosyncratic. They must intuitively appeal to those concerns of the audience which are shared; if they do not, the film's appeal is bound to be disastrously limited. As with pornography, the filmmakers have to create a work which is singular enough to fascinate and excite, and general enough to excite many. Moreover, in their search for the "hit," the ten to fifteen films out of the roughly seven hundred produced every year which evoke the most enthusiastic response, the filmmakers repeat and vary the daydreams as they seek to develop them into more and more nourishing substitutes for reality. Under the general rubric of fantasy, which can range all the way from the most primal images in dreams to the rationalized misinterpretations of reality in everyday life, the Hindi film is perhaps closest to the daydream. Indeed, the visual landscape of these films has a strong daydream quality in that it is not completely situated outside reality but is clearly linked to it. As Arjun Appadurai and Carol Breckenridge point out, while the landscape of the popular film contains places, social types, topological features, and situations which are reminiscent of ordinary experience, these elements are transformed or transposed so as to create a subtly fantastic milieu.[4] Even film speech is reminiscent of real speech. Thus the frequently heard admonition in "Indinglish," "Don't *maro filmi* dialogues, *yaar*," (Don't spout dialogues from films at me, friend), is often addressed to someone expressing highly inflated sentiments of friendship, love, or hostility which typify exchanges between the characters of Indian cinema.

Like the adult daydream, Hindi film emphasizes the central features of fantasy—the fulfillment of wishes, the humbling of competitors and the destruction of enemies. The stereotyped twists and turns of the film plot ensure the repetition of the very message that makes, for instance, the fairy tale so deeply satisfying to children—namely, that the struggle against difficulties in life is unavoidable, but if one faces life's hardships and its many, often unjust impositions with courage and steadfastness, one will eventually emerge victorious.[5] At the conclusion of both films and fairy tales, parents are generally happy and proud, the princess is won, and either the villains are ruefully contrite or their battered bodies satisfactorily litter the landscape. Evil in film, too, follows the same course it does in fairy tales; it may be temporarily in ascendance or usurp the hero's legitimate rights, but its failure and defeat are inevitable. Like the temptations of badness for a child who is constantly forced to be good, evil in Hindi cinema is not quite without its attractions of sensual licence and narcissistic pleasure in the unheeding pursuit of the appetites. It is usually the unregenerate villain who gets to savor the pleasures of drinking wine and the companionship, willing or otherwise, of sexy and attractive women.

Another feature common to both Hindi films and fairy tales is the oversimplification of situations and the elimination of detail, unless the detail is absolutely essential. The characters of the film are always typical, never unique, and without the unnerving complexity of real people. The Hero and the Villain, the Heroine and Her Best Friend, the Loving Father and the Cruel Stepmother, are never ambivalent, never the mixed ticket we all are in real life. But then, unlike in novels, the portrayal of characters in film is neither intended to enhance our understanding of the individual complexities of men and women nor to assist our contemplation of the human condition. Their intention is to appeal to the child within us, to arouse quick sympathies and antipathies, and thus encourage the identifications that help us to savor our fantasies more keenly.

When dogmatic rationalists dismiss Hindi films as unrealistic and complain that their plots strain credibility and their characters stretch the limits of the believable, this condescending judgment is usually based on a restricted vision of reality. To limit and reduce the real to that which can be demonstrated as factual is to exclude the domain of the psychologically real—all that is felt to be, enduringly, the actuality of one's inner life. Or, to adapt Bruno Bettelheim's observation on fairy tales, Hindi films may be unreal in a rational sense but they are certainly not untrue. Their depiction of the external world may be flawed and their relevance to the external life of the viewer remote; yet, as we shall see, in their focus on the unconsciously perceived fantasy rather than the consciously perceived story, the Hindi film demonstrates a confident and sure-footed grasp of the topography of desire. The stories they tell may be trite and limited in number, with simple, recognizable meanings which on the surface reinforce rather than challenge cultural convention. Yet beneath the surface, the fantasies they purvey, though equally repetitious, are not so trite and add surprising twists to the conscious social understanding of various human relationships in the culture.

Having described the relationship between Indian cinema, culture, and psyche in some detail, let me now turn to the cinema audience's internal theater of love as they watch the images flicker by on the screen. The composite love story I seek to present here is culled largely from a score of the biggest box office hits of the last twenty years.[6] Since it would be impossible as well as tedious to narrate the plots of all these films, I will take as my illustrative text only one film, Raj Kapoor's *Ram Teri Ganga Maili* (*Rama, Your Ganga is Polluted*), the top box office hit for the year 1986. I shall then use examples from other films to amplify and otherwise complete the prototypical love story of Hindi cinema.

Narendra, the hero of the film is a student of a Calcutta college and the son of a rich, thoroughly corrupt businessman. His father is a close associate of Bhag Choudhary, a villainous politician, whose only daughter, Radha, is romantically interested in our young hero.

Narendra, however, is unaware of Radha's feelings for him. He ignores her not-so-subtle advances and generally treats her in a friendly asexual fashion.

Narendra goes on a college trip to Gangotri, the source of the sacred river Ganges, in the Himalayan hills. He has promised to bring his doting grandmother pure Ganges water from the river's very source, since the water is polluted by the time it reaches the sea at Calcutta. He clambers down a mountainside to reach the stream, but the pitcher he has brought with him slips from his hand and rolls down the slope. As Narendra seeks to retrieve the pitcher, he is saved from falling over a cliff by a shouted warning from the heroine of the movie, Ganga. Ganga is a pretty, young girl of the hills, unspoilt and innocent, and frankly expresses her liking for the city boy. Often enough, she takes the initiative in their budding relationship. She leads him by hand on their excursions through the mountains, barefooted and impervious to the cold while he both stumbles and shivers. During their courtship they sing duets in meadows full of wild flowers and frolic through streams which, of course, make Ganga's thin white sari wet and cling revealingly to her well-formed breasts. Narendra saves Ganga from being raped by one of his college friends, which deepens the girl's feelings for the boy and increases their mutual attachment.

Although Ganga has been promised in marriage to one of her own people, she decides to break the engagement and marry Narendra. The marriage ceremony is preceded by a rousing (and arousing) folk dance and is succeeded by the wedding night. While inside the room, Narendra undresses Ganga with the gravity and devotion of a priest preparing the idol of the goddess for the morning worship, Ganga's brother and her enraged ex-fiancé are engaged outside in a murderous fight which will end in both their deaths.

Narendra goes back to Calcutta, promising to send for Ganga as soon as he has informed the family of his marriage. There he discovers that his grandmother has betrothed him in his absence to Radha, the politician's daughter, a match welcomed by both the families. After many emotional scenes involving the boy and his parents, in the course of which his grandmother suffers a heart attack and eventually dies, Narendra, defying his parent's wishes, sets out for the hills to fetch Ganga. By virtue of the political influence exercised by Choudhary, he is forcibly taken off the bus by the police before he can reach her village in the hills and is brought back to Calcutta.

In the meanwhile, a letter by Narendra's grandmother to her grandson reaches Ganga, from which she learns of the family's plans for

Narendra's betrothal; Ganga believes her husband now to be married to another woman. Their wedding night, however, has had consequences and Ganga gives birth to a child. Since, in Hindu tradition children belong to the father, Ganga nobly decides to take the infant son to far-off Calcutta and hand him over to Narendra. It is now that the perils of Ganga begin. Alighting from the bus at the foot of the hills and looking for the train station from where she can take the train to Calcutta, Ganga is instead guided to a cheap whorehouse. There she is sold to a customer who would rape her but Ganga manages to escape with the baby clutched to her breast. She then approaches an old priest for directions to the station. He, too, turns out to be lecherous. Ganga is saved from his attentions by the timely arrival of the police. Finally put on the train to Calcutta by a kindly police officer—who for a change does not try to rape her—Ganga is kidnapped on the way by a pimp who brings her to a *kotha* in Benares, a brothel whose customers are first entertained by song and dance in the traditional style of the Indian courtesan. Ganga becomes a well-known dancing girl though all the while retaining her mysterious purity, that "purity of the Ganges which lies in a woman's heart and which makes a man attracted to her, merge into her."

Ganga is now sold by the owner of the *kotha* to Choudhary who has come to Benares to find a girl to keep him company in his declining years. Choudhary, her husband's future father-in-law, installs the girl in a house in Calcutta and one day brings Narendra's father along with him to show off the girl's charms. He promises to share Ganga with him once the marriage of their children has been solemnized. On the day of the marriage, Ganga is called upon by Choudhary to entertain the wedding guests. As she sings and dances, Narendra recognizes her and without completing the marriage rites rushes to her side. His father and especially Choudhary and his goons try to stop him but Narendra and Ganga are finally united. Together with their infant son, they go away from the corruption of a degraded older generation toward a hopeful new future.

Superficially, *Ram Teri Ganga Maili* is a syrupy tale of the eternally pure woman whose devotion and innocence triumph over the worst efforts of lustful (mostly older) males to enslave and exploit her. As the third ear is deemed essential for listening in the analytic hour, similarly the analyst may need a third eye to break up the cloying surface of the film into less obvious patterns. Unlike Shiva's third eye which destroys all reality, the Freudian one merely cracks reality's stony surface to release its inner shape of fantasy. Like the dreamer who is not only the author, producer, and director of his dream but often plays all the important leads himself, the creator-audience of the film, too, is not limited to existing within the skin of the hero or the heroine but spreads out to cover other characters. The analyst may then reassign different values to the characters of the story than what has been the dreamer's manifest intent. He will, for instance, be mindful that besides experiencing the overt pity aroused by the hapless Ganga, the audience may well be deriving secret pleasure in the sexual villainy as well as surreptitiously partaking of the masochistic delight of her ordeals. Moreover, the third eye also destroys the very identities of the film's characters, replacing them with those of a child's internal family drama. Thus Ganga's screen image, with the infant clutched perpetually to her breast, becomes the fantasized persona of the mother from a particular stage of childhood. The faces of the various villains, on the other hand, coalesce into the visage of the "bad" aggressive father, forcing the poor mother to submit to his unspeakable desire. It is then with the third eye that we look at Indian men and women as lovers and at some of the situations and spaces of love they project on the screen.

Bearing a strong resemblance to another girl from the hills, Reshma, played by Nargis in Raj Kapoor's first film *Barsaat* four decades ago, Ganga is the latest reincarnation of the heroine who is totally steadfast in her devotion to a hero who is passive, absent, or both. Independent and carefree before being struck by the love-god Kama's flowery arrows, all that love brings her is suffering and humiliation, particularly of the sexual kind. Indeed, her suffering, like that of such legendary heroines as Laila and Sohni, seems almost a punishment for breaking social convention in daring to love freely. Rape, actual or attempted, is of course the strongest expression, the darkest image of the degradation she must undergo for her transgression.

The question why rape is a staple feature of Indian cinema where otherwise even the kiss is taboo, why the sexual humiliation of the woman plays such a significant role in the fantasy of love, is important. That this rape is invariably a fantasy rape, without the violence and trauma of its real-life counterpart, is evident in the manner of its visual representation. Villains, mustachoied or stubble-chinned, roll their eyes and stalk their female prey around locked rooms. With deep-throated growls of gloating, lasciviously muttering a variant of "Ha! You cannot escape now," they make sharp lunges to tear off the heroine's clothes and each time come away with one more piece of her apparel. The heroine, on the other hand, retreats in pretty terror, her arms folded across her breasts to protect her dishevelled modesty, pleading all the while to be spared from the fate worse than death. As in the folk theater presentations of the scene from the *Mahabharata* where Dushasana is trying to undrape Draupadi, what is being enjoyed by the audience is the sado-masochistic fantasy incorporated in the defencelessness and pain of a fear-stricken woman.

Now masochism is usually defined as the seeking of pain for the sake of sexual pleasure, with the qualification that either the seeking or the pleasure, or both, are unconscious rather than conscious. The specific locus of the rape fantasy for men is the later period of childhood which I have elsewhere called the "second birth," when the boy's earlier vision of the mother as an overwhelming feminine presence is replaced by her image, and that of woman generally, as a weak, castrated, suffering, and humiliated being. This is less a consequence of the boy's confrontation with female reality in the Indian family setting and more a projection of what would happen to him if he sexually submitted to the father and other elder males. As the boy grows up into a man, this fantasy needs to be repressed more and more, banished into farther and farther reaches of awareness. In the cavernous darkness of the cinema hall, the fantasy may at last surface gingerly and the associated masochistic pleasure be enjoyed vicariously in the pain and subjugation of the woman with whom one secretly identifies.

The effect of the rape scene on the female part of the audience, even if the movie rape is highly stylized and eschews any pretence to reality, is more complex. On one hand the sexual coercion touches some of her deepest fears as a woman. On the other hand, we must note the less conscious presence of a sexual fantasy due to the fact that the raping "baddies" of Indian cinema are very often older figures on whom the woman is dependent in some critical way: employers, *zamindars* (landlords), and so on. The would-be rapists in *Ram Teri Ganga Maili*, apart from the anonymous brothel customer, are the priest and the powerful Choudhary, the future father-in-law of Ganga's husband. In many other movies, the face of the father behind the rapist's mask is more clearly visible. Thus in *Karz*, a box office hit of 1979, the heroine's step-father stages a mock rape of his step-daughter to test the suitability of the hero as her future spouse. Wendy O'Flaherty has linked the power of this particular scene to the ancient myth in which the father-god (Brahma, Prajapati, or Daksha) attempts to rape his own daughter until she is rescued by the hero, Shiva.[7] She points out that this well-known myth is tolerated and viewed positively in Hindu texts which tell of the birth of all animal life from the incestuous union of father and daughter. I would, on the other hand—a case of cultural psychology complementing mythology—trace the woman's allurement in the fantasy of rape by the villainous father-figure to many an Indian woman's adolescence. This is perhaps the most painful period of a girl's life, in which many renunciations are expected of her and where her training as an imminent daughter-in-law who must bring credit to her natal family is painfully stepped up. Psychoanalysis regularly brings up the powerful wish from this period for an intimacy with the father in which the daughter is simultaneously indulged as a little girl and treated as a young woman whose emerging womanhood is both appreciatively recognized and appropriately reacted to. In part, this is a universal fantasy among women, arising from the fact that a father often tends to withdraw from his daughter at the onset of puberty, feeling that he should no longer exhibit physical closeness, doubtless also because of the sexual feelings the daughter arouses in him. The daughter, however, learning to be at home in a woman's body and as yet insecure in her womanly role, may interpret the father's withdrawal as a proof of her feminine unattractiveness. The wished for father-daughter intimacy becomes a major fantasy in India because of the fact that in the Indian family the father's withdrawal from his daughter is quite precipitate once she attains puberty. The daughter is completely given over to the woman's world which chooses precisely this period of inner turmoil to become increasingly harsh. The rape by the father is then the forbidden, sexual aspect of her more encompassing longing for intimacy. The fearful mask worn by the father is a projection of the daughter's own villainous desire which frees her from the guilt for entertaining it.

Narendra, the hero of the movie, is a passive, childlike character, easily daunted by his elders who put obstacles in the path of the lovers' union. He is a pale shadow of the more ubiquitous romantic hero who suffers the despair of separation or disappointment in love with a suprahuman intensity (by which I mean less that of an inconstant god than of the faithful child lover). Such a hero used to be very popular in Indian films until about twenty years ago. Since in India nothing ever disappears, whether religious cults, political parties, or mythological motifs, the romantic lover too lives on, though at present he is perhaps in the trough rather than at the crest of the wave. For my generation, however, the images of this lover, as played for example by Dilip Kumar in *Devdas* or Guru Dutt in *Pyasa*, remain unforgettable.

The Majnun-lover, as I would like to label this type after the hero of the well-known Islamic romance, has his cultural origins in a confluence of Islamic and Hindu streams. His home is as much in the Indo-Persian *ghazal* (those elegies of unhappy love where the lover bemoans the loss, the inaccessibility, or the turning away of the beloved) as in the lover's laments of separation in Sanskrit and Tamil *viraha* poetry—of which Kalidasa's *Meghaduta* (*The Cloud Messenger*) is perhaps the best-known example.

Elsewhere, I have discussed the psychological origins of the Majnun-lover as part of the imperious yet vulnerable erotic wishes of infancy.[8] His is the wish for a total merger with the woman; his suffering, the wrenching wail of the infant who finds his budding self disintegrating in the mother's absence. What he seeks to rediscover and reclaim in love is what is retrospectively felt to be paradise lost—the postpartum womb of life before "psychological birth," before the separation from the mother's anima took place. These wishes are of course part of every man's erotic being and it is only the phallic illusion of modern Western man which has tended to deny them legitimacy and reality.

All soul, an inveterate coiner of poetic phrases on the sorrows and sublimity of love, the romantic lover must split off his corporeality and find it a home or, rather, an orphanage. The *kotha*, the traditional style brothel, is Hindi cinema's favorite abode for the denied and discarded sexual impulses, a home for vile bodies. Sometimes replaced by the shady night club, a more directly licentious import from the West, the *kotha* provides the alcohol as well as the rhythmic music and dance associated with these degraded impulses. Enjoyed mostly by others, by the villain or the hero's friends, for the romantic lover the sexual pleasures of the *kotha* are generally cloaked in a pall of guilt, to be savored morosely in an alcoholic haze and to the nagging beat of self-recrimination.

The Krishna-lover is the second important hero of Indian films. Distinct from Majnun, the two may, in a particular film, be sequential rather than separate. The Krishna-lover is physically importunate, what Indian-English will perhaps call the "eve-teasing" hero, whose initial contact with women verges on that of sexual harrassment. His cultural lineage goes back to the episode of the mischievous Krishna hiding the clothes of the *gopis* (cow-herdesses) while they bathe in the pond and his refusal to give them back in spite of the girls' repeated entreaties. From the 1950s Dev Anand movies to those (and especially) of Shammi Kapoor in the 1960s and of Jeetendra today, the Krishna-lover is all over and all around the heroine who is initially annoyed, recalcitrant, and quite unaware of the impact the hero's phallic intrusiveness has on her. The Krishna-lover has the endearing narcissism of the boy on the eve of the Oedipus stage, when the world is felt to be his "oyster." He tries to draw the heroine's attention by all possible means—aggressive innuendoes and double entendres, suggestive song and dance routines, bobbing up in the most unexpected places to startle and tease her as she goes about her daily life (Jeetendra is affectionately known as "jack in the box"). The more the heroine dislikes the lover's incursions, the greater is his excitement. As the hero of the film *Aradhana* remarks, "Love is fun only when the woman is angry."

For the Krishna-lover, it is vital that the woman be a sexual innocent and that in his forcing her to become aware of his desire she get in touch with her own. He is phallus incarnate, with distinct elements of the "flasher" who needs constant reassurance by the woman of his power, intactness, and especially his magical qualities that can transform a cool Amazon into a hot, lusting female. The fantasy is of the phallus— Shammi Kapoor in his films used his whole body as one—humbling the pride of the unapproachable woman, melting her indifference and unconcern into submission and longing. The fantasy is of the spirited androgynous virgin awakened to her sexuality and thereafter reduced to a groveling being, full of a moral masochism wherein she revels in her "stickiness" to the hero. Before she does so, however, she may go through a stage of playfulness where she presents the lover a mocking version of himself. Thus in *Junglee*, it is the girl from the hills—the magical fantasy-land of Indian cinema where the normal order of things is reversed—who throws snowballs at the hero, teases him, and sings to him in a good-natured reversal of the man's phallicism, while it is now the hero's turn to be provoked and play the reluctant beloved.

The last fifteen years of Indian cinema have been dominated, indeed overwhelmed, by Amitabh Bachchan who has personified a new kind of hero and lover. His phenomenally successful films have spawned a brand new genre which, though strongly influenced by Hollywood action movies such as those of Clint Eastwood, is neither typically Western nor traditionally Indian.

The Bachchan hero is the good-bad hero who lives on the margins of his society. His attachments are few but they are strong and silent. Prone to quick violence and to brooding periods of withdrawal, the good-bad hero is a natural law-breaker, yet will not deviate from a strict private code of his own. He is often a part of the underworld but shares neither its sadistic nor its sensual excesses. If cast in the role of a policeman, he often bypasses cumbersome bureaucratic procedures to take the law in his own hands, dealing with criminals by adopting their own ruthless methods. His badness is not shown as intrinsic or immutable but as a reaction to a developmental deprivation of early childhood, often a mother's loss, absence, or ambivalence toward the hero.

The cultural parallel of the good-bad hero is the myth of Karna in the *Mahabharata*. Kunti, the future mother of the five Pandava brothers, had summoned the Sun when she was a young princess. Though her calling the Sun was a playful whim—she was just trying out a mantra—the god insisted on making something more of the invitation. The offspring of the resulting union was Karna. To hide her shame at Karna's illegitimate birth, Kunti abandoned her infant son and cast him adrift on a raft. Karna was saved by a poor charioteer and grew up into a formidable warrior and the supporter of the evil Duryodhana. On the eve of the great battle, Kunti approached Karna and revealed to him that fighting on Duryodhana's side would cause him to commit the sin of fratricide. Karna answered:

> It is not that I do not believe the words you have spoken,
> *Ksatriya* (warrior caste) lady, or deny that for me the
> gateway to the Law is to carry out your behest. But the
> irreparable wrong you have done me by casting me out has
> destroyed the name and fame I could have had. Born a
> *Ksatriya*, I have yet not received the respect due a baron.
> What enemy could have done me greater harm than you
> have? When there was time to act you did not show your
> present compassion. And now you have laid orders on me,
> the son to whom you denied the sacraments. You have
> never acted in my interest like a mother, and now, here you
> are, enlightening me solely in your own interest.[9]

Karna, though, finally promised his mother that on the battlefield he would spare all her sons except Arjuna—the mother's favorite.

The good-bad Bachchan hero is both a product of and a response to the pressures and forces of development and modernization taking place in Indian society today and which have accelerated during the last two decades. He thus reflects the psychological changes in a vast number of people who are located in a halfway house—in the transitional sector—which lies between a minuscule (yet economically and politically powerful) modern and the numerically preponderant traditional sectors of Indian society. Indeed, it is this transitional sector from which the Bachchan movies draw the bulk of their viewers.

The individual features of the good-bad hero which I have sketched above can be directly correlated with the major psychological difficulties experienced by the transitional sector during the course of modernization. Take, for instance, the effects of overcrowding and the high population density in urban conglomerations, especially in slum and shanty towns. Here, the lack of established cultural norms and the need to deal with relative strangers whose behavioral cues cannot be easily assessed compel the individual to be on constant guard and in a state of permanent psychic mobilization. A heightened nervous arousal, making for a reduced control over one's aggression, in order to ward off potential encroachments, is one consequence *and* a characteristic of the good-bad hero.

Then there is bureaucratic complexity with its dehumanization which seems to be an inevitable corollary of economic development. The cumulative effect of the daily blows to feelings of self-worth, received in a succession of cold and impersonal bureaucratic encounters, so far removed from the familiarity and predictability of relationships in the rural society, gives rise to fantasies of either complete withdrawal or of avenging slights and following the dictates of one's personal interests, even if this involves the taking of the law into one's own hands. These, too, form a part of our hero's persona.

Furthermore, the erosion of traditional roles and skills in the transitional sector can destroy the self-respect of those who are now suddenly confronted with a loss of earning power and social status. For the families of the affected, especially the children, there may be a collapse of confidence in the stability of the established world. Doubts surface whether hard work and careful planning can guarantee future rewards or security. The future itself begins to be discounted to the present[10]. The Bachchan hero, neither a settled family man nor belonging to any recognized community of craftsmen, farmers, etc., incorporates the transitional man's collective dream of success without hard work and of life lived primarily, and precariously, in the here-and-now.

The last feature of the portrait is the core sadness of the good-bad hero. On the macro level, this may be traced back to the effects of the population movements that take place during the process of economic development. The separation of families, the loss of familiar village neighborhoods and ecological niches, can overwhelm many with feelings of bereavement. Sometimes concretized in the theme of separation from the mother, these feelings of loss and mourning are mirrored in the Bachchan hero and are a cause of his characteristic depressive detachment, in which the viewers, too, can recognize a part of themselves.

As a lover, the good-bad hero is predictably neither overtly emotional like Majnun nor boyishly phallic like the Krishna lover. A man of controlled passion, somewhat withdrawn, he subscribes to the well-known lines of the Urdu poet Faiz that "Our world knows other torments than of love and other happinesses than a fond embrace." The initial meeting of the hero and heroine in *Deewar*, Bachchan's first big hit and widely imitated thereafter, conveys the essential flavor of this hero as a lover. The setting is a restaurant-night club and Bachchan is sitting broodingly at the bar. Anita, played by Parveen Babi, is a dancer—the whore with a golden heart—who comes and sits next to him. She offers him a light for his cigarette and tells him that he is the most handsome man in the bar. Bachchan, who must shortly set out for a fateful meeting with the villain, indifferently accepts her proffered homage as his due while he ignores her sexually provocative approach altogether. Indeed, this narcissistically withdrawn lover's relationships with his family members and even his best friend are more emotionally charged than with any woman who is his potential erotic partner. Little wonder that Shashi Kapoor, who played the hero's brother or best friend in many movies, came to be popularly known as Amitabh Bachchan's favorite heroine!

Afraid of the responsibility and effort involved in active wooing, of passivity and dependency upon a woman—urges from the earliest period of life which love brings to the fore and intensifies—the withdrawn hero would rather be admired than loved. It is enough for him to know that the woman is solely devoted to him while he can enjoy the position of deciding whether to take her or leave her. The fantasy here seems of revenge on the woman for a mother who either preferred someone else—in *Deewar*, it is the brother—or only gave the child conditional love and less than constant admiration.

The new genre of films, coexisting with the older ones, has also given birth to a new kind of heroine, similar in some respects to what Wolfenstein and Leites described as the masculine-feminine girl of the American movies of the 1940s and 1950s.[11] Lacking the innocent androgyny of Krishna's playmate, she does not have the sari-wrapped femininity (much of the time she is clad in jeans anyway!) of Majnun's beloved either. Like the many interchangeable heroines of Bachchan movies, she is more a junior comrade to the hero than his romantic and erotic counterpart.

Speaking a man's language, not easily shocked, she is the kind of woman with whom the new hero can feel at ease. She is not an alien creature of feminine whims, sensitivities and susceptibilities, with which a man feels uncomfortable and which he feels forced to understand. Casual and knowing, the dull wholesomeness of the sister spiced a little with the provocative coquetry of the vamp, she makes few demands on the hero and can blend into the background whenever he has more important matters to attend to. Yet she is not completely unfeminine, not a mere mask for the homosexual temptation to which many men living in the crowded slums of big cities and away from their women-folk are undoubtedly subject. She exemplifies the low place of heterosexual love in the life of the transitional man, whose fantasies are absorbed more by visions of violence than of love, more with the redressal of narcissistic injury and rage than with the romantic longing for completion—a gift solely in the power of a woman to bestow.

Having viewed some dreams in Indian popular cinema with the enthusiast's happy eye but with the analyst's sober perspective, let me reiterate in conclusion that *oneiros*—dream, fantasy—between the sexes and within the family, does not coincide with the cultural propositions on these relationships. In essence, *oneiros* consists of what seeps out of the crevices in the cultural floor. Given secret shape in narrative, *oneiros* conveys to us a particular culture's versions of what Joyce McDougall calls the Impossible and the Forbidden,[12] the unlit stages of desire where so much of our inner theater takes place.

4

The Sex Wars

There is a certain kind of popular narrative in India which neither consists of the folk version of stories from the pan-Indian epics nor of legends based on local events and motifs. Widespread over large linguistic regions, this narrative has a specific form, where the mundane is not separated from the supernatural.[1] With a frame-tale as its starting point, the narrative comprises loosely connected stories within stories, a format made famous by *A Thousand and One Nights*.

In spite of a profusion of magical happenings, these narratives are closer in spirit to the folktale than to the myth. They too fulfill the folktale's psychological function of neutralizing the archaic, alloying ambivalence with humor, alleviating anxiety through playfulness, and demonstrating clear-cut pedagogical intentions. The last is accomplished by portraying specific patterns of behavior which are registered unconsciously by the reader or the auditor till a corresponding situation arises in his life. Recalling the story, he can then recognize the pattern as it applies to his own predicament, thus enhancing his feeling of conscious mastery and expanding the borders of his observing ego.[2]

Printed in cheap paperbacks in thousands of copies every year, and easily available at the pavement bookstalls of bazaars in both small towns and larger cities, these books are also a part of the literary offerings at well-known temple complexes where they routinely jostle Hindu theogonies, prayer collections, descriptions of rituals, and shiny scrolls with colored illustrations of the various tortures of hell. Sporting a jacket cover of pure kitsch, generally in faded reds, blues, and yellows which have run into each other on the low-quality paper used for their production, these books are printed in an unusually large type—known as Bombay type in the Hindi speaking heartland and *periya elutta* (literally "large script") in Tamil—for the instruction and entertainment of men and women at the edge of literacy and also uncertain of the availability of sufficient illumination at night.

Exclusively focusing on the relationship between the sexes, *Kissa Tota Myna* or *The Story of the Parrot and the Starling* is one such popular collection of fourteen tales in Hindi. Although of poor literary quality, *Tota Myna* may nonetheless claim a noble ancestry in *Sukasaptati*, a twelfth-century collection of tales on the unfaithfulness of women, told by a parrot to a merchant's wife to guard her chastity while her husband was away. Like its counterparts in other languages, for instance *Matankamarajan Katai* in Tamil, *The Parrot and the Starling* has an abundance of magical and supernational trappings and eschews description and reflection in favor of a fast forward (and sideward) movement of the story. Its characters are preeminently princes, princesses, and courtiers from kingdoms of never-never lands. It's language, though undemanding, is nevertheless ornamented with well-known couplets and folk sayings from both Hindi and Urdu, reflecting the interpenetration of Hindu and Muslim streams in the mass culture of northern and central India from which this narrative derives.

The frame tale of *Kissa Tota Myna* is of a parrot who alights upon the branch of a tree one evening seeking a place to rest for the night. The tree is home to a starling, militantly feminist in her own way, who demands that the parrot fly off immediately. The starling cannot bear the thought of sharing her night abode with a member of a sex she hates for its cruel and unfaithful nature. The exhausted parrot defends the male sex and levels counter allegations against the female of the species. As evidence for their respective positions, each bird then tells a succession of tales which, taken together, last for fourteen nights. The following story, eighth in the series, is quite typical for both the literary poverty and the cultural-psychological richness of the whole collection.

The parrot said "O Myna! A city called Kanchanpura was ruled by a king Angadhwaja and his queen Chandraprabha. The queen was virtuous and devoted to her husband. One day a brahmin came to Angadhwaja and gave him two pieces of paper. On the first piece it was written, 'A king who stays awake all night achieves great results.' On the second: 'Whoever honors an enemy has all his transgressions forgiven.'

"King Angadhwaja put both pieces of paper in his pocket and sent away the brahmin after honoring him with a gift of money. After a few days the king wanted to test the truth of the brahmin's words. One night, after finishing all his work, he decided to stay up till the morning. While the king was awake in his palace, he heard a woman crying outside. The king felt great pity for the woman and thought to himself that there were unhappy people dwelling in his city. 'I must go at once and find the cause of her unhappiness,' he said to himself. For the *dharma* of the ruler demands that he take part in the sorrows and pleasures of his subjects, punish according to the crime and look after his people as if they were members of his own family.

"Arming himself fully the king walked towards the sound of weeping and found a hundred-year-old woman sobbing loudly. 'O Mother! What makes you so unhappy that you are crying at midnight?' the king asked.

" 'O traveler! Why do you interfere? Go your way. The cause of my suffering cannot be removed by the Creator himself let alone by a man,' the woman answered.

" 'At least tell me what makes you so sad,' said the king.

" 'I'll tell you only if you never repeat it to anyone for otherwise you'll be turned into stone,' the old woman replied.

"The king agreed to this condition and the old woman said, 'Son, tomorrow night at ten, Angadhwaja, the king of this city, will be bitten by a snake and die. That is why I'm crying. Where will we ever again find such a virtuous king?'

" 'O Mother, just as you have told me the reason for your weeping, kindly also tell me from where this snake will come,' the king said.

" ' Son, outside the western gate of this city there is a temple of Shiva. Near the temple there is a banyan tree and the snake lives in a hole at the root of the tree. The snake is an enemy of the king from its previous birth and now wishes to avenge itself for the earlier enmity,' the old woman said.

" 'Mother, tell me also why the snake is an enemy of the king?' the king asked.

" 'Son, this king was a merchant called Manisen in his last incarnation and his wife was named Kesar. She was twenty years old and very beautiful. One day Manisen went off to a distant land on business leaving Kesar at home with an eighteen-year-old servant. In his absence the lord of love, Kama, sorely afflicted Kesar's body and her fancy turned toward the young servant. She called the boy, asked him to sit on the bed with her and frankly expressed her desire for him. The boy folded his hands and said, "O merchant's daughter! I shall never perform the act with you since I have heard from elders that a person who feeds and clothes you is like a parent and a man who does the bad act with his mistress goes to hell." Hearing the boy, Kesar said, "It will go badly with you if you do not make love to me." She threatened him in various ways but the boy was adamant. After some days when

Manisen returned, the wife thought that she would get into trouble if the boy ever told the husband what had transpired while he was away. So she thought of something which would both protect her and punish the boy for the insult he had offered her.

" 'When Manisen came home he found his wife sad. "O Beloved! why are you lying listless today?" "O Lord! You have returned. Now take care of your house because I am going to kill myself," Kesar replied. "What is your unhappiness that you want to give up on life?" Manisen asked. "Lord, I have no sorrows for your glory has given me all possible happiness. But in your absence your servant did me grievous injury and you must punish him, otherwise I shall die," Kesar said. "What did he do to you? Tell me frankly," Manisen said.

"O Lord! One night as I was sleeping on the roof he climbed up on my bed, seated himself on my breasts and wanted to do the bad act with me. But I awakened and seeing him astride my body I cried out aloud and only then did he leave me. On hearing my screams people came up, but out of shame I could say nothing to them. Only God protected my virtue that night," Kesar said. Hearing this, Manisen became red with anger and said, "O my beloved! Why be unhappy? Have your bath, eat, and enjoy yourself. The boy shall be punished this very night for what he has done to you." When night fell, Manisen stabbed the boy repeatedly with a knife and buried the body in his courtyard. Manisen has been now reborn as the king and that boy is reborn as a snake who seeks vengeance.' On hearing this the king went back to his palace."

The parrot said, "O *Myna*! Think about it. What was the poor boy's fault that the woman did not have any pity on him and had him murdered?" The starling replied. "In this affair both the man and woman are at fault since the man killed the youth merely on the say-so of his wife without further inquiring into the matter." The parrot said, "O *Myna*! I have already said earlier that when a woman in her attractive form embraces a man and infatuates him with her sweet words and desire's arrows then the man loses all his reflective power."

"Let me reply to that," said the starling.

"First let me finish my story and then you may give your reply," said the parrot.

"When the king returned to his palace he could not fall asleep because of worry. His hand went to his pocket and he found the second piece of folded paper given to him by the brahmin. He opened this and read therein that one's enemy should be honored. He said to himself, 'What the brahmin wrote down on the first scrap of paper certainly came true. Let me also try out his second piece of advice. At the moment

I have no other enemy than the snake so I must show him all respect.[2] In the morning he called his chief minister and other courtiers and told them that a snake would come to bite him that night. 'So you should clean up the road from my bed to the snake's hole. Sprinkle the whole way with perfume and rose petals and line it with cups of perfumed milk,' he instructed.

"When the time came, the snake, full of anger, emerged from its hole and started moving towards the king's palace. But it was completely captivated by the perfume and the rose petals lining its way. In whichever direction it turned there was delicious milk to be drunk. In its contentment the snake said to itself, 'This king, knowing me to be his enemy, still looks after me so well. I shall not bite him. I must go and tell him that I have forsworn my revenge.' When the snake entered the king's bed chamber the minister reached for his sword. But the king forbade him from drawing the weapon. He then extended his hand and said, 'O Lord Serpent! Now take your revenge by biting me.'

" 'Glory be to you, O king, and glory to the parents who have sired such a courageous and virtuous son. I am very pleased with you and shall not harm you.' So saying the snake went away.

"On seeing all this the people were amazed. Then the queen addressed her husband thus, 'O King! Please tell me how you knew about the snake?'

'O Queen! I cannot do so because the person who told me warned me that I shall be turned to stone if I ever revealed the secret,' the king replied. 'Whether you turn into stone or not, you must tell me the story otherwise I shall give up my life,' said the queen. The king was very upset for he loved his wife dearly and could not bear to be without her for even a moment. He was so blinded by his love that he did not reproach her for her stubbornness and only said, 'Well, if I must turn into stone I shall do so at the banks of the river Ganges. Then, as a stone, I shall at least lie in the sands of the holy water.'

"The king then prepared to proceed to the Ganges. The king's servants and many others from the city accompanied him on his journey. His minister tried to reason with him saying, 'If there is life you'll get many other queens. You are otherwise so sensible yet are bent on losing your life because of a woman's whim.' But the king was so infatuated that he did not heed this wise counsel. Then the minister went to the queen and said, 'O Queen! Renounce this willfulness so that the king's life may be saved. If he reveals the secret and turns into a stone where will you again find such a king? Will his successor give you any

respect? Every headstrong woman has always suffered for her willfulness.'

" 'Which woman has paid for her stubbornness? Tell me the story of
even one such woman.' said the queen.

"The minister said, 'O Queen! There was a city called Sursen ruled
by King Rupadutta, who was very handsome. His wife, Chandrakanta,
was very beautiful, but she had become immoral even before her
marriage. When she came to her husband's home after marriage she
brought her lover along with her in the guise of an eunuch. During the
king's absence in his court she enjoyed herself with the lover. One day
the king came to know this and he tried to reason with the queen. But
the queen said, "I have given my heart to my lover. You can do what you
like but I shall never give him up." The king had both her ears and her
nose cut off and banished her from his city while the eunuch was
hanged. The woman who does not listen to her husband always comes
to a bad end. Now leave this stubbornness of yours because your
husband is a king and no one can ever be sure of a king's moods. Some
poet has rightly said:

A king, a yogi, fire, and water
Have a contrary nature
One should always avoid them
For their affections are uncertain.

But the queen remained adamant in her wish to know the king's secret
and the hapless minister retreated.

"In the morning they all left the city and at noon came to a river where
the king rested. He went to the river to wash himself and saw a herd of
goats come to the stream to drink water. All the goats left after slaking
their thirst except for one who saw a fruit floating on the current. The
goat wanted the fruit badly. When the billy goat saw that one goat
remained behind, he asked her the reason for not joining the others. The
goat answered, 'If you get me the fruit from the river I'll come with you
otherwise I shall not move.'

"' What if I drown?' asked the billy goat.

"' Whatever happens I will not move without the fruit,' was the
reply. The billy goat was furious. Eyes red with anger, it said, 'You
don't know me well enough. I am not a fool like King Angadhwaja who,
infatuated with a woman, goes to the Ganges to lay down his life.' It
then started butting the goat till she rejoined the herd.

" 'The billy goat's remarks went straight to the king's heart, who said to himself, 'I am even lower than a goat in my infatuation. Today I realize that the queen whom I love so much is hungry for my very life. Some poet has indeed rightly remarked:

A woman is a mother to give birth
A girl, for intercourse
A goddess, to receive worship
And death, to take life back.'

The king said to himself, 'I am a big fool. Fie on my intelligence! Fie on women who control men by their sweet words and fie on those men who lose everything and become slaves to these bundles of wickedness!' He then called his minister and the queen and said, 'O Queen! I shall now tell you the secret and then become a stone. What is your wish?'

" 'O King! whatever may happen, you must tell me the secret,' the queen answered. The king then picked up a whip and thrashed the queen. She begged forgiveness but the king was implacable. He called his executioners and told them to pluck out the queen's eyes and leave her in the jungle. The executioners followed the orders and the queen received due punishment for her deeds."

The parrot said, "O *Myna*! The race of women is indeed not to be trusted."

The starling answered. "O Parrot! Do not exaggerate, I too can tell you of the unfaithfulness of men."

The next night, in reply, the starling tells the story of four princes who got lost while hunting in a forest. When they finally emerged from the forest they came to a city inhabited by sorcerers. After wandering around in the city the princes sought out an inn where they could rest for the night. The innkeeper was a sorceress who had four beautiful daughters. The girls were infatuated with the princes and at night had them carried to their rooms through their magic. The three older girls turned three princes into sheep whom they fed well during the day and then transformed back into men at night for the purpose of sexual enjoyment . The youngest daughter, however, fell in love with the youngest prince and kept him as a man without employing any magic spells at all. Their love grew so much that they could not stay apart for a moment. One day, the youngest prince became very sad as he sorely missed his parents. On being asked the cause for his sadness he told the girl about the unhappiness being caused to his parents at the separation from all their sons. He asked her to employ her skills in sorcery so that the brothers could be released from their enthrallment and go back to their parents. He further suggested that she too accompany him back to his father's kingdom where they would be married and she become a princess. In her devotion to the man, the young sorceress followed his wishes, thus earning the wrath and vengefulness of her sisters. She fled the city together with her lover and his brothers. On the way to the prince's kingdom, while resting for the night in a forest, the youngest prince deserted the sleeping girl. After many tribulations, the sorceress reached her lover's city and wanted to be together with him again. He, however, threw her into prison for the night and had her hanged in the morning.

Of the many narrative forms, the folktale, it seems to me, is closest in reflecting the concerns of the ego of the Freudian tripartite model, an ego which mediates between the instinctual desires of the id and the imperatives of the superego. In the folktale, the primitive aspects of the id and the superego are relatively underplayed. The analysis of the folk tale would then ideally keep closer to the surface of the text. In addition, the analyst would look for a single fantasy (in contrast to the novel where fantasies are generally multiple) which would help him structure the surface elements of the tale into a new pattern, revealing a new emphasis.

A major feature of the *Tota Myna* stories is the marked lack of any tender feeling or mutuality between men and women who move across their pages as if they were members of different species altogether. At the conclusion of each tale, one of the lovers is routinely mutilated, stabbed, thrown alive in a well, or decapitated by the other, with the female more likely to meet a bloodier end than the male. The stories can be more correctly described as erotic fantasies of hatred than love, the hostility and aggression between the sexes far outweighing any affectionate promptings.

In the tales, the male perception of the woman as an erotic partner is of a sexually voracious being who is completely ruled by the dictates of her body. Especially vulnerable to the power of eros, the phrase *jab uske sharir ko kamdeva ne sataya* ("when her body was sorely troubled by the god of love") is used solely in connection with a woman, never a man. She is the initiator of sexual advances and loses all sense of proportion and moral constraints when in the grip of erotic passion. At such times, in her quest for sexual satisfaction, she would blithely sacrifice her parents, husband, or children. When sexually intoxicated, the woman takes one lover after another without discriminating between young and old, handsome and ugly, rich and poor. In many tales, women perversely favor fakirs and yogis as lovers, doubtless also because the disheveled "holy" men, with their unkempt beards and matted hair, are fantasized by Hindus and Muslims alike to be possessors of great virility, capable of satisfying the most insatiable of women. It goes without saying that women are also deceitful and unpredictable, with motivations that are an enduring puzzle to men. As one of the folk proverbs in a story puts it, *Triya charitra na jane koye, Khasam mar ke sati hoye.* ("No one knows the character of a woman; she will first kill her husband and then mount the funeral pyre as a sati.")

Elsewhere, I have traced this view of the woman's rampant, heedless sexuality to the "sexual mother" of early childhood.[3] She is a figure of male imagination, constructed from the boy's perception of an actual maternal eroticism, heightened in the Indian context, combined with the projection of his own desire toward her. The sorceress who uses the prince for sexual enjoyment at night while she turns him into a helpless sheep during the day—night being the diurnal home of fantasy and imagination—the merchant's wife who, Phaedra-like demands that the servant boy gratify her desire or risk severe retribution, are two of the many masks of the "sexual mother" which women wear in these tales. The "Oedipal" fantasy of many stories is further underscored by the lovers women serve or choose in preference to and in betrayal of the hero. Often enough the lover is a fakir and yogi who, as Robert Goldman suggests in the case of the guru in legends from Sanskrit epics, may well be a substitute for the father who lays sexual claim to the mother.[4]

Although most stories mark the passage of the Freudian mother in the man's fantasy, there are also a couple of tales which herald the appearance of the Kleinian one; the defence against the anxiety around genital sexuality being replaced by reassurance against the earlier "oral" fears of devouring and being devoured by the mother. In one story, for example, a goddess fries a king in oil every night, eats his flesh and then the next morning sprinkles nectar (*amrita*) on the bones by which he is resurrected in his original form. In return for this service, the king daily receives a large quantity of gold from the gratified goddess.

The female perception of man in *Tota Myna* is of a creature of short-lived passions whose only experience of love is lust. Once erotic passion retreats and lust is satisfied, the man is revealed as a being full of guilt who will unceremoniously desert the woman he has loved to distraction only a short while earlier. The man's guilt is chiefly toward the parents for his desertion of them in order to initiate adult sexual relations. In one story after another, the hero proves to be vastly more attached to his parents than to the beloved. Given the perception of the man as someone who is infantile in his attachments, volatile in his affections, and cruel in his anger, the woman's choice in love, the stories seem to suggest, is limited to appeasement and masochistic surrender.

Serpents as Lovers and Spouses

In literature, folklore, myth, ritual, and art, the snake and especially the cobra (*nag*) plays a prominent role in Hindu culture. Born of one of the daughters of Prajapati, the Lord of Creation, snakes are carried by Shiva, the Destroyer, around his neck and arms, while there is no more popular representation of Vishnu, the Preserver of the Hindu trinity, than of his reposing on the Sesha, the seven-headed cobra. Sculpted into the reliefs of Buddhist, Jain, and Hindu temples, snakes, both single and entwined, are a ubiquitous presence in Indian sacred space. On a more mundane level, *nag* is a popular name among both men and women and *naga-panchami*, the festival of snakes on the fifth day of the Bhadon month in the rainy season, is celebrated all over India with the ritual worship of the cobra.

One would therefore expect that the motif of the snake lover, of both men and women, is widespread in popular Indian narrative, and this expectation is not belied. This motif can trace its antiquity to the myths of the *Mahabharata* where the great ascetic Jaratkuru married the sister of Vasuki, the king of snakes. The redoubtable warrior-hero Arjuna, too, married Ulipi, Vasuki's sister, and bedded a serpent princess during the one year of his banishment.[5] The first tale of the snake lover that I would like to narrate and interpret here is the second part (quite unconnected with the first) of the story of Princess Standing Lamp. This story, well-known as a folktale in other parts of South India, is part of a Tamil collection of tales mentioned earlier in the chapter, *Matankamarajan Katai—The Story of King Matanakama*—and my version is condensed from the English translation of Kamil Zvelebil.[6] The section of the story I reproduce here commences after the marriage of the princess and the prince, a time when they should have "lived happily ever after." But it so transpires that the prince becomes infatuated with another woman with whom he spends his days and nights, completely neglecting his young bride.

For three years, things went on like this. Then one day an old woman who happened to be the neighbor of the princess came to see her and said: "Dear child! You are quite young and pretty, and yet your husband is a whoremonger! What kind of wife is she who is unable to control her husband?"

"What can I do, mother?" complained Standing Lamp. "Since Brahma has created me like this, nothing can be done against it!"

"So, Brahma has created you like this, has he?" answered the old woman in mockery. "Don't say foolish things! It is your own fault that you suffer! But if you listen to my advice you won't regret it!" And when the princess agreed to listen, the old woman proceeded: "Here, take this magic drink and mix it with the *rasam* (spiced lentil soup) prepared for your husband! He won't leave you for a second!"

Taking the magic drink with apprehension, the princess thought: "I wish I knew how this works! If she is right, we will be happy as before. But suppose that it harms him. What shall I do?" And, being unable to make up her mind, Standing Lamp went out and spilt the magic drink in her backyard, serving her husband an innocent usual *rasam*.

A snake lived in an old anthill in the backyard, and a few drops of the *rasam* mixed with the love potion fell on its head. As a result, the snake became infatuated with the princess. As soon as her husband left for the house of the *dasi* (female servant), the enamored serpent tapped at Standing Lamp's door. She went to see who it was. As she opened the door, she was happy to behold her husband come back! The snake had taken the form of the prince. Without further hesitation, she gave herself to the snake, who enjoyed her fully in its embrace.

The princess carried on thus with the serpent for some time, and as a result became pregnant. When the snake came to know of her condition he felt a desire to tell her the truth. The serpent said: "Woman! I am not your real husband! Your husband is at this moment in the house of the *dasi*. I am the five-hooded snake living at the back of your house. The love potion which your neighbor, the old woman, gave you the other day, fell on me, and as a result I came to love you. But now I am going to break the infatuation which your husband feels for the *dasi* who plays the role of his wife."

After a short time, the prince, still infatuated with the *dasi*, found out that his wife was with child. He ran to his father-in-law and complained that his wife, the princess, must have been unfaithful to him, since although he had not touched her for some two years, she was pregnant!

The king sent a few maids to bring his daughter to his presence. Standing Lamp sought the advice of the snake.

The serpent, coiled in the bed of the princess, laughed and said: "Your bad days are over. When the king, your father, asks about your condition, tell him without any fear whatsoever that your husband alone is the father of your child. If there should be any doubt, turn to the members of the court and tell them that you are willing to undergo any test in the temple or before any deity. Don't be afraid! Or better still, say this: Bring a pot and let in a serpent. I'm willing to put my hand into the pitcher with the snake to retrieve a gold coin placed inside! In this way, no one will doubt your word. I shall of course manage to be the snake in the pitcher!" And the serpent left.

As soon as the sun rose, the princess got up, dressed in her best attire and jewels, and appeared in the hall of audience of the royal palace. The king turned to his son-in-law and said: "Well! Why don't you ask her what you wanted to ask her?"

"Sir," said the prince-husband, "how is it that when it is two or three years since I last touched her, this woman is now bearing a child?"

Standing Lamp addressed the gathering of councillors: "I am indeed pregnant, and no one else but my husband is the father. If you have any doubt, I am willing to undergo the ordeal by snake!" The king and the prince and the members of the council agreed, and a snake catcher was immediately sent for and asked to produce a suitable cobra.

The snake catcher came and started to play his flute. The five-hooded snake king subdued all other snakes, and entered the pitcher that had been prepared, with a golden coin dropped inside.

The princess had a bath, and as soon as she returned she went round the pot and uttered the following words: "The one whom I touched on my wedding day was truly my husband; today I shall truly touch the serpent." Then she removed the seal from the pot, thrust her hand inside, took out the snake, threw it round her neck like a garland, removed the gold coin, deposited it on a golden platter—and the father and the husband, and the ministers cheered her, shouting: "She is indeed a *maha pativrata*, utterly chaste and faithful and a great lady!" All of them praised her virtue, while she returned home, and the prince had no more doubts that he must be the father of the child.

The *dasi* was curious; she sent her servants to the princess with the request that she should bring her child for her to see. "Our mistress must see your baby! Please, give it to us!" Standing Lamp told them to come on the next day. The servant girls returned without the baby, and the offended *dasi* reported to the prince what had happened. "What? I send for my son and she dares to refuse? What is this?" And he promptly complained to his father-in-law the king about the conduct of his wife.

That night Standing Lamp called the serpent and asked him: "The *dasi* asked for our son. What shall I do? Shall I send him to her?"

The snake replied: "Finally it has happened. Good days are ahead of you now. Your husband will return to you, and the *dasi* will this time lose his affection. Deck the child with all ornaments and send him to your father. When they come to fetch him, weigh the child along with jewels. Tell them that they should return him precisely as he is. If the weight will be less, the *dasi* will not only have to make good the loss but also become your slave. The jewels of the child will be made of *nagaratna*, the snake-gems, and even your father's entire treasury will not equal them in value. I'll come, and snatch away the jewels. Don't be afraid, and send the child without worry!"

Next morning, the king's servants came to the princess: "Lady, your father our lord the king wants to see you." The princess took the child and appeared in the king's presence. "Daughter," said the king, "your husband wishes to see his son!" When she remained silent, he went on: "Why haven't you sent the child to him?" Standing Lamp answered: "Sir, I have no objection to send my boy to the house of the *dasi*. All I fear is that he may be robbed of his precious jewels. I therefore humbly submit that he is weighed here and now along with his jewels. If he is returned intact and in the same weight, I shall be satisfied. However, if something is missing, I insist that the *dasi* be dispossessed and become my slave. If she agrees to this, I'm willing to send my child along."

The king summoned his son-in-law and the *dasi*. They accepted the conditions. The princess placed her son in a cradle, in another cradle she placed the jewels and she had them weighed so that everyone could see and have no doubt. The *dasi* then took the boy and the jewels to her house, fondled the child, caressed it, played with it, fed it with milk, and kept it with her for the night.

In the dead of the night, the serpent crawled in, and in utter secrecy stole away some of the most precious jewels.

In the morning, Princess Standing Lamp insisted that the child and the jewels be weighed in the presence of the king and the councillors. It was at once revealed that the weight of the jewels had diminished! The councillors watched everything carefully and decided: "The *dasi* is guilty of a crime. The jewels have been stolen. The *dasi* must act according to the agreement." Without the least contradiction the *dasi* became a servant in the household of the prince. The princess was happy. After some time, she was restored to her husband's affection, and while the *dasi* took their orders as their domestic slave, they enjoyed life to the full.

In this new-found joy, the princess completely forgot the snake. The snake thought: "Ah! Oh! Because of us, the princess has found new happiness, and now she has forgotten us! However if we bite and kill her, there won't be any joy in that for us! We cannot make love to her now. All that is gone. The best solution for us is to commit suicide!" And it decided to strangle itself with a lock of Standing Lamp's hair.

So, one night, the snake crawled into her bed, and entangling itself in a lock of her hair, died on the spot.

The next morning, at sun-rise, the young ruler woke up and was horrified to find a dead snake in his wife's hair! As he woke her up, her head was heavy with the weight of the dead snake, so large was it. She was afraid even to move, but she felt terrible remorse and sadness. She realized why it had killed itself. "Why do you weep?" asked the husband. "O lord of my soul! This is our home snake. I had prayed to him and offered *puja* (worship) to him for your return to me! But when you did return, I forgot all about him! That's why he came, and died!" And she added: "Please, take the boy, and perform the rites, and have the snake cremated prayerfully with due obsequies."

The prince agreed. With the assistance of the boy, he performed obsequial ceremonies for the snake and had it burnt. They worshipped the snake regularly.

From them on, Princess Standing Lamp, the young king, and the boy lived happily together.

This shows that women are not to be trusted in this world! They are a tricky and deceptive lot.

The serpent as a lover of the human female virtually *demands* an interpretation of the snake's symbolic significance. This demand cannot be evaded even when we know that it is the area of symbolism which has earned psychoanalysis its greatest opprobrium and harshest criticism. Viewed by some as akin to a crankish medieval bestiary, the Freudian theory of symbols has been accused by its critics of ignoring the all-important context in its quest for ferreting out a universal sexual significance of natural objects and artifacts. The accusation has some substance although it was Wilhelm Stekel rather than Freud who introduced the notion of a one-to-one correspondence between the symbol and the symbolized. Taken over by Freud and incorporated in the second and subsequent editions of *The Interpretation of Dreams*, the notion of universal symbolism, in fact, contradicts Freud's own dream theory.[7] Whatever its uneasy place in theory, we know that in his clinical work, an analyst, of whatever persuasion, proceeds from and remains closely connected to the uniqueness of his patient's "text." There is neither a straightforward application of theory from a cookbook of interpretations nor any culling out of facile equivalences from some lexicon of universal symbols that can help the analyst understand and interpret the meaning of the analysand's communications.

The impression that the psychoanalytic theory of symbolism is based on a kind of invariance and is indifferent to context perhaps stems from its historical evolution where, in the early years, the Oedipal period was regarded as the fulcrum, both of mental life and of symbol formation. Thus the child's use of the representation of his own body parts to symbolize his conflicted relationship with a parent—the cutting off of hair to symbolize castration anxiety, to take an example, is then limited to analytical material from the Oedipal context. In later periods of development, the "castration anxiety" may be expressed in symbols of loss of identity or of humiliation which do not necessarily involve a mutilation of body parts. Conversely, one symbol may express more than one idea and it is the various details and minutia of the context which determine whether a given image is symbolic and what exactly it is symbolic of.

This caution is especially necessary in the case of the snake, which traditionally has been a symbol with multiple meanings. In religious beliefs around the world, the snake is both accursed and worshipped. Repository of all mysteries, representative of the chthonic powers of the underworld, epiphany of the moon, a symbol both of immortality and the threatening powers of death, symbolically the snake occupies a unique position in the animal world.[8]

Psychologically, too, depending upon the context, the snake can symbolize a variety of meanings.[9] Because of some of its real or perceived characteristics—extending itself, swelling and rearing up the head (cobra), penetrating into holes and crevices in the earth, secreting a fluid, evoking the tacky and clammy sensation associated with genitals—the snake has been traditionally considered the most important symbol of the male organ. There are, however, other contexts in which the snake is not a phallic symbol. Evoking its hidden aspects and the more python- rather than cobra-like associations of enveloping, strangling, incorporating, and swallowing small creatures, the snake can come to symbolize a devouring vagina, a dangerous femininity; its poison—a death in the coital embrace. In yet other contexts, it can be equated with the umbilicus which is a bridge to the womb, while its characteristic of sloughing off the old skin in exchange for a new one can come to represent change and transformation, the hope of psychic rebirth in therapy. It is then through the configuration of three contexts—of the narrative, of the culture, and of the symbolism associated with the snake, that we can arrive at a more careful interpretation of the serpent lover of our tale.

The situation in which a newly married bride competes with another woman for the affections of her husband is not particularly novel in narratives of Indian gender relations. The theme of the *souten*, a co-wife or a mistress who rules the man's heart and must be dislodged from this position, is the subject of many folktales as well as songs. In most tales, we are told the wife wins back her husband's love by being patient, virtuous, and clever.[10] She tricks her rival into revealing her flaws which puts her own attractiveness in sharp relief. The fantasy of the serpent lover, however, involves deeper layers of the woman's psyche. In psychoanalytic parlance, it contains more id than ego material, which is generally true in folktales. The serpent lover appears in reaction to Princess Standing Lamp's grievous disappointment in the prince at the beginning of their married life. The snake provides her with the status of motherhood which, for an Indian girl, consolidates her identity as a woman and can mean a significant improvement in her position in the politics of joint family life. The snake is the elusive fulfillment of both a romantic and social quest. It is the "good penis," the idealized phallus of the woman's fantasy. This interpretation is fully consistent with the cultural symbolism of the snake where the worship of god-like *naga* deities is closely linked to sexuality and reproduction and is also supported by the serpent's more universal phallic significance. We can see some of the underlying dynamics in this fantasy in a clinical vignette.

A twenty-five-year-old woman has been deeply worried about her husband's evident romantic interest in another woman. She dreams that the man tells her he is going to spend the weekend with this woman. She protests violently, but her protestations have no effect on the man who goes off on his tryst. A group of gods, dressed as bandits, of whom she is not sure whose side they are on, follow the man. When she comes to the house where the husband has gone, she finds him lying dead on a hospital bed, his body badly mutilated, evidently killed by the bandit gods. Sitting on the man's body is a wonderful snake, glistening, glittering, and studded with diamonds, and toward whom she feels a strong attraction.

In the story, of course, the murderous rage felt by Princess Standing Lamp toward her philandering husband is completely absent, whereas in the dream it is half-heartedly sought to be disavowed by the device of the bandit-gods who may or may not be on the woman's side, that is, may or may not be a part of her. Yet the outcome in both the dream and the story, the replacement of the disappointing real-life husband by an idealized serpent lover, is strikingly similar.

The snake lover of our story differs significantly from the animal groom tales of Western folklore which have been a subject of psychological analysis by Bruno Bettelheim.[11] In a reversal of the Indian pattern, the Western sexual partner is first experienced as an animal, a human being who has been turned into a loathsome beast by a sorceress. He is not a product of the heroine's disappointment in marriage. She is forced to join him while still a maiden because of her love or obedience to the father, and it is her devotion to her animal lover that disenchants him and gives him back his human form. Bettelheim interprets the European fairy tale as a message for the girl that to achieve a happy union the female has to overcome her view of sex as loathsome and animal-like. In my own interpretation of the snake lover as an idealized phallus, it may well be that idealization helps the girl overcome her childhood fears of the adult male organ which can lacerate and "bite" into her insides. The "good penis" helps her in the acceptance of a violation of her body's boundaries, a violence inherent in the sexual act. The snake, after all, figures prominently in threats of chastisement directed toward the female child in some parts of India. But more important, given the radical changes in a girl's situation brought about by marriage and the overwhelming nature of demands made on her by her new family, coupled with an inattentive or straying husband, the private yet culturally shared fantasy of the idealized phallus both consoles and eases her transition.

The psychic transformation required in giving up the dreams of girlhood and settling into the reality of married womanhood then require the unconscious fantasy of the "good penis." Whoever this phallus may ultimately belong to—the father, a god, the ideal male—it can only serve as a transitional object. The snake, strangled in her tresses at night while she sleeps, must die as must her earlier dreams of love and passion before she can settle into conjugal domesticity and motherhood. Both the snake and the "good penis"—the one is the other—are then perpetually mourned in the secret recesses of her heart, their memory now incorporated in the son.

My story of the snake *wife* derives from the arena of popular, mass culture. It is the 1987 movie, *Nagina*, said to be an all-time top grosser in the history of Indian cinema. Raju, the twenty-one-year-old hero of the movie, returns home after a fifteen-year sojourn in England. He is the only son of a wealthy mother—his father having died while he was away—who was sent to England as a child to be treated there for inexplicable anxiety attacks. Raju was cured and stayed on with his uncle in London, where he grew up and went to school.

During his absence, the family's considerable estates were looked after by a friend of his father's, the movie's first villain, who would like his daughter to be married to Raju. Encouraged by the mother, who is not averse to this proposal, the young man takes the girl out on a buggy ride. On the way he narrowly misses being bitten by a cobra which, coiled around the rear axle of the buggy, follows him home and is witness to the mother's love and distress at the danger her son has just escaped.

The next day Raju visits the ruins of the house in which he had spent the first six years of his life. Here, among the ruins which have a powerful emotional impact upon him, he hears a female voice singing a song with the refrain:

A forgotten story is remembered
An old memory surfaces again.

Through the mist which swirls among the ruins, Raju gets tantalizing glimpses of the singing woman—the back of her head, a shoulder, a foot tapping in rhythm to a dance—and he follows her. Finally, he comes face to face with a beautiful young woman who tells him that they had spent a lot of time together in the ruined house in the past. Raju, in spite of his best efforts, cannot remember. He continues to meet Rajni ("Night"), which is her name, and duly falls in love with her.

In the meanwhile, the villain has received Raju's mother's consent to the hero's marriage to his daughter. Raju, though, protests and persuades his mother to change her decision in favor of Rajni. The villain vows revenge for this slight. He sends one of his henchmen to murder Rajni, but two cobras, who are the girl's protectors, kill the would-be assassin. The villain then arranges for a gang of bandits to attack Raju's house on the day of his wedding to Rajni, but the cobras bar the bandit's way and the marriage takes place as scheduled.

The villain now refuses to hand back Raju's property; the documents in which he had acknowledged Raju's ownership have been misplaced. But Rajni, who the audience by now knows is an *ichhadhari* cobra— a snake who, in Indian serpent lore, as a reward for many hundred years of ascetic practices, can assume any form at will—locates the missing documents through her paranormal vision. The villain and his men waylay Raju with the intention of killing him. Rajni again protects her husband and the villain dies, bitten by the cobra.

Much more dangerous to the couple, however, is the arrival of the family's guru, an evil *tantrik* (the practitioner of an esoteric Hindu cult) who possesses formidable occult powers. Immediately on entering the family mansion, he discerns the presence of a cobra and recognizes Rajni to be a snake woman. However, before he can do anything he is ordered out of the house by the unsuspecting Raju who looks down upon *tantriks* and gurus as purveyors of old-fashioned religious mumbo jumbo.

The guru sends his own pet cobra to bite Raju, who is convalescing in a hospital room from injuries received in the fight with the villain. Rajni, who is watching over her sleeping husband, resumes her snake form and kills the guru's cobra after a fierce struggle. She then warns the guru from trying to harm Raju, maintaining that her powers gained through her devotion to her husband are as great as the guru's undoubted ones.

The guru now informs Raju's mother about the real nature of her daughter-in-law. He tells her to keep a close watch on Rajni who must resume her original snake form once every twenty-four hours. The old woman does so and sees for herself Rajni changing into a cobra at night. She rushes to the guru for help. The evil guru tells her that she should get her son out of the way on the day of the snake festival, when he would come to their home and carry away the snake bride whom he needs for his own purposes. She is his lead to a *nagmani*, the mythical snake ruby supposedly found in the head of a rare *ichhadhari* cobra, whose possession will make him the most powerful man on earth.

Rajni, who knows of her mother-in-law's visit to the *tantrik*, seeks to dissuade her from seeking the guru's help. She tells Raju's mother that she has come to their home to love and protect the son and means the family no harm. In a series of flashbacks, she reminds Raju's mother of the day when her son was bitten by a snake on his sixth birthday. The boy was dead but was revived by the *tantrik* guru, who took out the snake's life and put it into Raju's body. The snake who thus died in return for the child's life was Rajni's husband and she had vowed revenge. But on seeing the closeness between mother and son, she had relented and decided on Raju as a husband. The frightened mother-in-law, however, chooses to follow the guru's wishes and on the day of *naga-panchami* sends Raju away from home on some pretext.

Now follows what has been popularly regarded as the movie's highlight: Rajni's "snake dance." Clad in saffron robes, a string of beads around his neck, the guru enters the hallway along with four of his similarly attired disciples. They start playing the *been*, the thick wooden flute pipes used by snake charmers, whose sound is supposed to be irresistible, drawing out snakes from the most hidden nooks and crannies. In an upstairs room we see Rajni dressed in a sequined, tight-fitting white dress which emphasizes her large breasts and swelling hips. As the strains of the *been* come floating into the room, Rajni feels impelled toward the sound in a snake-like slithering movement. Her hands cupped over her head in a cobra's hood, she sashays down the spiral staircase. Dancing toward and away from the men, all jiggling breasts and writhing hips, the *beens* of the men looming large over her body in close-ups and then retreating, the guru's face reflecting a cold, determined lust, Rajni is dancing her way into an apparently reluctant yet clearly willing sexual surrender. The spell is broken by the unexpected return of Raju who slaps his wife for her "shameless" dancing. Rajni runs away to the ruins, followed by the guru who, in turn, is followed by a furious Raju. There is a long drawn-out fight betweeen the two men, in which Raju's mother is killed while protecting her son. The guru is finally bitten by the cobra but before dying repents of his evil desires and prays to Shiva to release Rajni from her snake incarnation into a human one. The prayer is granted and both Raju and Rajni live happily ever after.

Nagina is, of course, also a traditional folk narrative, though with many additions and modifications to suit contemporary Indian conditions which encompass certain modern, essentially Western, elements. Just as many scholars claim that in India, in contrast to Europe, there are no hard and fast boundaries between folk and classical traditions, both of which share a common base and thus are different aspects of the same tradition rather than separate traditions,[12] similarly I believe Indian popular mass culture also cannot be clearly delimited from its folk and classical counterparts. Popular culture, too, exists in continuity, almost a flux, with other cultural forms, and is part of the same basic tradition to which it provides fresh subject matter and new impetuses.

The story of *Nagina* can be "read" from many perspectives. A more sociological reading, for instance, will perhaps emphasize the critique of modernity implicit in the persona of the naive hero whose Western-style rationality is utterly ignorant of the hidden mysteries of the occult realm accessible only to traditional knowledge. Our more psychological reading, though, focusses exclusively on the symbolic reverberations of the snake woman figure, both in the plot of the movie and in the larger tale of Indian gender relations.

Raju's first encounter with the snake woman already points in the direction we should look for her meaning. Singing of forgotten, that is, repressed memories in the ruins of the house where Raju had spent the first six years of his childhood and which he feels impelled to visit again and again, emerging from and retreating into mists of the past, the snake woman, I would suggest, incorporates a particular "vision" of the mother from the earliest years of the boy's life. She is not a passive, long-suffering paragon of maternal love, which is the way the real mother is portrayed in the movie and the way "Mother" is consciously perceived by men in most Indian narratives. A more unconscious construction, this mother is utterly sensual yet fiercely protective. She is both the seductive dancer and the hissing, spitting cobra fighting to protect the boy from all who would harm him. She is the desired mother of the six-year-old's willful fantasy to whom a villainous father, in the shape of the guru, also lays sexual claim, and whose adult virility she can barely (and perhaps does not even want to) resist. Saved from the "evil" designs of the man by the boy, she helps the son vanquish the father so that they can live blissfully united together in an age-old boyhood dream.

5

Husbands and Others

To cynics, love, the core of gender relations, is the opiate of the privileged classes; its relevance for lives of the destitute, locked in a struggle for sheer survival, minimal. Suspicious of romanticism, old or new, they believe that the "culture of poverty" (to use Oscar Lewis's telling phrase[1]), generates its own compulsions in the very poor, which override the ideals, values, and prescriptions of the traditional culture of their society which in any case is preeminently an elite creation.

The following autobiographical accounts from the slums of Delhi try to give voice to the hopes, wishes, fantasies and conflicts of two women who belong to a group which is otherwise ignored and rarely heard from in the largely middle- and upper-class discourse on the relationship between the sexes. The self-narratives of Janak and Basanti are vibrant tales whose allusions and nuances can only be imperfectly conveyed in any English translation of their tape-recorded interviews. In narrating their first-person stories, my primary intent is to recreate a sense of the "who" in the lives of two individual women enmeshed in a web of relationships. As an analyst who is also professionally aware of the fate that befalls an interrupter of tales, I would ideally have the reader fully enter Janak and Basanti's stories before I come in with my own interpretations. My endeavor is to guard against the reader's *experience* of the two women being prematurely foreclosed by *explanation*.

Yet going beyond their individual fates, the women's tales invariably also tell us something about gender relations in Indian lower-class life and in the culture of the larger society to which they both belong. Before letting them speak in their own voices, I shall abstract some of the features they share with other lower-class Indian women and compare them with other women, both in the higher strata of Indian society and in the urban slums of some other parts of the world.

Together with many others from the "resettlement colony," home to some of the poorest of the poor of Delhi, Janak and Basanti have a gift for self-description, even self-dramatization, once their initial mistrust of a stranger is replaced by a confidence in the stranger's empathic intentions. They are neither inarticulate nor does their language operate according to a "restricted code" (as compared to a supposedly more "elaborate" code of middle- and upper-class language) which is said to be the characteristic of lower class speech in the West.[2] Often crude and vulgar by middle-class standards, their language reflects accurately the women's animation and their utter involvement in the drama of their own lives. With a marked lack of preparation in utterance, there is yet a kind of zany fluency in the language which is liberally sprinkled with analogies, allusions, and proverbs from the dominant Hindu culture from which the women have not been separated by poverty. Thus when Janak, talking of what she swears are her husband's unjustified suspicions about her sexual morals, says "I wished the earth would split open to swallow me," she is referring to the well-known episode from the *Ramayana* where the epic's heroine, Sita, placed in a similar predicament, called upon her mother Earth, to open up and take her innocent daughter back into herself.

The culture penetrates many other areas of their lives. Janak and Basanti are not strangers to the rituals and the *vratas* (the ritual days of fasting) prescribed for Indian women, and have followed the Hindu blueprint for a woman's dealings with the supernatural, for instance, when one is possessed by a spirit or a goddess.

The stamp of the traditional culture is clearest in shaping their ideals of the "good" woman, especially in relationship to a man. They share with women of the higher classes the feelings of being loved and approved of by a watchful inner sentinel when conforming to this ideal, and stabbings of guilt when they deviate, as sometimes they must. The "good" woman, of course, is a daughter whose premarital chastity and steadfastness to the monogamous ideal in thought, word, and deed is the repository of her parental family's honor (*izzat*). The "good" woman is naturally fertile, particularly in the matter of giving birth to all-important sons. Her failure in this regard can lead to banishment from hearth and home, a punishment which may be resented yet is also accepted as just for her betrayal of the ideal.

Above all, in the ideals of the traditional culture, the "good" woman is a *pativrata*, subordinating her life to the husband's welfare and needs in a way demanded of no other woman in any other part of the world with which I am familiar. The *pativrata* conduct is not a mere matter of sexual fidelity, an issue of great importance in all patriarchal societies.

We can understand the underlying male concerns when in the *Mahabharata*, the goddess Uma, laying down the guidelines of right conduct for women describes a *pativrata* as one, "who does not cast her eyes upon the Moon or the Sun (both male in Hindu cosmology) or a tree that has a masculine name." The goddess, however, goes further,

> Devotion to her lord is a woman's merit; it is her penance; it is her eternal heaven. Merit, penances, and Heaven become hers who looks upon her husband as her all in all, and who endowed with chastity, seeks to devote herself to her lord in all things. The husband is the god which women have. The husband is their friend. The husband is their high refuge. Women have no refuge that can compare with their husband, and no god that can compare with him. The husband's grace and Heaven, are equal in the estimation of a woman; or, if unequal, the inequality is very trivial. O Maheshwara, I do not desire Heaven itself if thou are not satisfied with me. If the husband that is poor or diseased or distressed were to command the wife to accomplish anything that is improper or unrighteous or that may lead to destruction of life itself, the wife should without any hesitation accomplish it.[3]

This "right conduct" for the wife, repeated over and over again in the major repositories of the cultural tradition, builds a part of the Hindu woman's "ideology of the superego." With varying degrees of intensity it cuts through all strata of Indian society. The echoes of the *pativrata* wife will also be heard in the accounts of women from the slums who often invoke the name of Sita, the personification of the *pativrata* ideal, and allude to one or another episode of her mythological life.

The problem, of course, is that unlike the spouse of most women in the higher classes, the slum husband is apt to be shiftless. For all practical purposes, the lower-class woman frequently finds herself abandoned and in charge of the family even if her abandonment does not reach the degree and proportions met with in the ghetto families of, say, New York. The imperatives of physical protection, economic support, and the quieter need for male companionship lead her to establish more or less permanent liaisons with other men. Such unions and consensual marriages inevitably force cracks in her inner image of the good woman, faithful to one man not only through this life but in all subsequent ones. Sexual promiscuity is not a consolation or a compensation she readily permits herself for her many deprivations, unlike her sisters from slums of some other parts of the world. Like other Indian women, she too recoils from seeking a sexual remedy for injuries inflicted by life.

The woman from the Delhi slum is like her counterparts in other slums of the world in that there is a high degree of physical violence in her relationships with men; mutual suspicions of sexual infidelity being the apparent cause for frequent explosions. She, too, is more tolerant of hedonistic entrancements (except those of sex) which make spontaneity and enjoyment still possible in the daily grind for survival. She, too, has developed a fortitude and an ability to cope with problems that would leave women from the middle-and upper-classes helpless.

Where she differs from women of other urban slums is in an enduring intimate connection with the traditional culture in her inner life and in her close, tangible ties with the natal family. Indeed, the support she receives from her parents, brothers and sisters, would be the envy of other Indian women who are expected to forego this source of aid and succor and deal with the exigencies of married life on their own. Thus the slum woman rarely feels marginal, isolated, or dependent, and only occasionally helpless.

Her connectedness to the cultural tradition and the family also help in shielding her from the realities of her situation when these become too grim. It provides her raw material for fantasy in her poignant yet determined struggle to maintain self-respect as a "good" woman. One major fantasy, protecting her from feelings of depression and rage, is of the heroine, battered by fate and men, finally triumphing both through her suffering and her commitment to virtue. In the last act which fantasy obligingly conjures up on her inner screen, the man will be abjectly contrite as he realizes her true worth, his brutishness transformed into adoration. The grown-up children, mindful of the mother's sacrifices on their behalf, will be devoted to her needs and welfare. And in the heavenly aisles the gods, no longer indifferent, will give her a standing ovation as they shower her with flowers and looks of pride.

[The translations of the following narratives are my own.]

Janak

We have lived in Madangir since the last 17–18 years. Earlier we stayed in Gandhinagar. We were three sisters and two brothers. After coming to Delhi from Pakistan as refugees we stayed with relatives. My father was very poor. We ate two *rotis* (North Indian bread) in the evening and then went to sleep. There was never a third one. When we sisters wore clothes or plaited our hair, people used to say, "Their father is so poor. Where do they get money for clothes?" We wore clothes only when someone gave us old ones. My father was mostly unemployed. I was the eldest child in the house. When my father came home in the evenings he was always in a bad state. My heart ached for him. The other sisters did not care.

When I was in the tenth class in school, a man used to visit our house. I asked him to get me a job as a village welfare worker. (I have never told this to anyone before but am telling you now.) He said he would do it. This man used to deal in girls from an office in front of the Irwin Hospital. I was clever and alert from the very beginning. He took me to the office and around seven in the evening brought me to a deserted spot in Shahadra where there is now a cremation ground. God saved me. The man said, "Take off your clothes." I took off my new sandals which I had got from Lucknow. Then I said to him, "I will take my clothes off." I had to trick him. I said, "Step back a little, so I can strip without shame." He thought he had trapped me. I untied the string of my trousers, dropped them and ran. Wearing just a shirt I came back home naked, but he had not succeded in touching me. I cried and cried. My parent's honor was almost plundered that day and it was only God who gave me the strength to save it. The man brought my sandals and my trousers back because he knew my father was poor. My parents collapsed on the floor. In those days I kept all the *vratas*—and went to the temple every day.

For the training as a village welfare worker, I went to Durgapur near Simla. I did not even have a uniform. A contractor I had come to know said he would buy me one. But his eye was evil. Look, if a person is poor then everyone looks at her with bad intentions. He brought me two saris, a pair of shoes, and blouses. I had to travel alone that night. The contractor asked me to marry him because his wife was not a good woman. I told him, "I have called you 'brother' so I cannot look at you in that way." Then I got on the train but felt sad during the whole journey.

I wanted to help my father financially. I felt homesick in Durgapur. I contracted smallpox and my skin erupted with boils. After a year I came back home. Mother had taken to bed. The other sisters did not look after her, so after returning I got her treated. I was very fond of my brothers and sisters. I would have liked them to be educated but they wanted to take the evil path. The parents were respectable people, but the children betrayed their trust.

Now I am fifty years old. I was seventeen when I was married to Premnath in Gandhinagar. He is a distant relative and in those days he was in the army in Allahabad. Once when he visited our home my father asked him to look me up in the village near Nainital since I was living alone in foreign parts. When he finally found me I welcomed him with great respect. His looks changed then. He thought he'd be happy if he could marry me. Such a thought never entered my head. Then he went back to Allahabad and wrote me a letter, asking me to marry him. But I said this was not possible since we were related.

Should I tell you the truth? I went to Allahabad to meet him. When he came to the station to see me off he cried and cried. He was very handsome in those days and I liked handsome men. His complexion was fair and he spoke so sweetly and softly that if a third person was sitting nearby he couldn't make out what the man was saying. He had so much politeness. I forgot everything after meeting him. I said to myself that I must have him for my very own. His mother had died when he was a child. He wept often, saying he had no one. I forgot everything after seeing his loneliness. I did not see any of his inner qualities. I thought about him day and night. We both used to write verses and songs to each other in our letters. We said we couldn't live without each other.

When I came home for a vacation I told my mother about him. He took leave from his job and came to our house one day and just sat there. He said if he couldn't get married to me he would knife everyone. My father took off his turban and placed it on my feet and said "Child, keep my honor and refuse him. He is a very bad man. He will ruin your life." I said "No, if he is a bad person then it is in my hands to make him good." I said to my father, "So what if he kills me! You'll carry my corpse to the cremation ground on your shoulders." My father married me off but when I was about to leave home he hid himself. He said, "She has done this against my will, she has not listened to me. I will not see her when she leaves. She was the one who was my son, but she has now betrayed me." So my *doli** went to my sister's house since my husband had no money for us to go anywhere else.

When he left me to go to Allahabad he promised to send money. My parents began to hate him. They said he has got married and left his wife

---

* The groom's carrying away the bride from her father's home in a ritual procession.

which is a matter of great dishonor. So they also harassed me. I wrote him a worried letter and without letting him know came to Allahabad. We took a room from one of his friends and spent a very good year. We were together all the time: I never slept alone for even one night. Then I became pregnant. My health worsened. The vomiting would not stop. So in the eighth month he brought me back to my mother. My baby was about five weeks old when he ran away from the army but said that he had come on leave. One day passed, two days passed. Whenever the girl cried he would say, "Come, let's throw her into the Jamuna river. Throw the sister-fucker into the river!" Neither the child nor I had anything to eat. At home the parents would say, "What was the great pleasure in getting married when there is no money. He is nothing but a naked, starving beggar!" I could not tolerate this and so we shifted to my sister's shanty in Link Road. We got a hut of our own but did not have enough money even for milk for the child. By this time he had started beating me with a whip.

The baby became very weak and died when it was four months old. We brought her to Irwin Hospital and they put four bottles of glucose into her but she could not be saved and died by the morning. He began to be upset with our lack of money. I would tell him, "I will always be with you. I have left my parents, I have left my brothers and sisters, left all my relatives, I am with you." Then my sister got him a job in Eros Cinema for a hundred rupees a month.

One night what happens is that he has gone to the cinema. Taking my younger sister—she died sometime ago—we looked for him the whole night. When he came home at four in the morning he was drunk. I said to him, "Listen, I searched for you the whole night." He did not say anything. He took off his boots and hit me hard with one of them. Four, five times, on the head. Who was I to question him if he had been with a woman! When a man's character goes bad he will always hit the woman. He locked me in the hut and went off. The same day the police came to demolish our huts. They loaded us and our belongings in trucks and threw us out here in Madangir which was then just an empty, dusty plain. I was alone. When my brothers came to know, they came looking for me. They asked what had happened. I told them that their brother-in-law had left me. They spent the whole day clearing up a space, digging foundations, making a hut for me.

Eventually, he came back. Every day he would harass me, beat me. By this time I had another child, almost fifteen months old. He would take a knife out in front of the child and say that he'd kill me. My mother often said, "Leave him, his character is bad. You will weep your whole life." But I said, "No, I have taken hold of his hand. He is my consort. You may all leave me but I shall never leave him." He made scenes. Abuses, beatings, staying away from home. When I was sick he'd never ask whether I needed a cup of tea or milk. He'd often say, "I will throw you down the roof." But he is my husband. And then my son died when he was a year and a half old.

You know, when I was a child my father told me many stories. Two of these stories have stayed in my mind. In a village the daughter of a brahmin and the son of another brahmin loved each other. The brahmin boy asked the girl to run away with him and one night they took off. On the way they stopped to rest in the veranda of a house. Two thieves who had just robbed a house came to the place where the couple was sleeping. They were followed by the villagers who cornered them in the veranda. The villagers asked the girl which one was her husband. The brahmin boy was a weakling while one of the thieves was a strong and handsome young man. Besides, he also had money and jewellery. The girl did not take a moment to change her mind. Ignoring the brahmin boy, she identified the thief as her husband and went away with him. On the way they came to a river and wondered how to cross it. The thief said, "Let me first go and leave the bag on the other side and then I will come back and carry you across." When he reached the other shore the girl called him to come back and take her with him. He said "When after choosing a man you left him so easily, how can I trust you to stay with me?" So my father told me that a woman belongs to one man only. If she is going to get happiness then it is only from him, never from someone else. A husband is God.

Another story I liked a great deal is about a king who had five daughters. He made them sit in a row and asked, "Who gives you the food you eat?" All the daughters except one said, "Father, you give us the food." The fifth daughter said, "Father, I eat what is given by God, what is given by my *karma*." The king was furious. He called a leper, bleeding from his sores, married this daughter to him and turned her out of the palace in rags. While leaving the girl said, "O Father! This is the husband of my *karma*—this husband is my god!"

She began begging to feed her husband, patiently broke pieces of bread and put them in his mouth. He would ask her not to waste her youth on him and to marry someone else. "God has made me to serve you," she always replied. One day, leaving him in the jungle, she went off to the town to beg. A bird came and sat on the tree under which the leper was resting. The bird said to the leper, "My prince, there is a pond nearby. If you bathe in its waters your leprosy will disappear." The man

72

dragged himself to the pond and put one leg in the water. It was cured instantly. He put in another leg which also became clear of all disfigurement. He dipped his whole body and came out clean, like a golden king. When the girl came back, she did not believe this handsome man was her husband. He convinced her by putting his little finger, which had not touched the water earlier, into the pond and showing her that it had become clean. The bird came again and said "If you boil two cans of oil and put the oil in the pond the water will part and you will find at the bottom treasures buried by ten kings." The couple followed the bird's instructions and built a big palace for themselves from the gold and the gems.

One day the husband said to the wife that we must call your father for dinner. When the king came the daughter served him, wearing a new dress and jewellery with every dish. When the king finished eating she came out with the rags in which her father had turned her out. She then presented her husband to him and said, "These are the clothes you gave me and you have seen the clothes given by my *karma*. You gave me a leper for my husband and this is the man *karma* has given me."

Look, no one can erase even one line of what *karma* has written down in your book. My man could not be mine. I do not understand why. But my lack of understanding does not mean that I should leave good *dharmic* (according to the law) thoughts and embrace bad ones? You can get peace only from your own man, not from others.

We had been hiding in shanties for five years while the warrants for his arrest for desertion from the army were out. One day finally the police came and took him away to Banga in Punjab. I followed him to the police station, crying all the way. They took him to jail in the military cantonment in Jullundhar. I stayed there for twenty-one days and went to see him each day. He would abuse me every time I came and I would cry.

I loved him. I loved him so much that mother-father, sisters-brothers, the whole world was of less worth to me than my man. I could not leave him. I said if he is sent far away from me I will die. They gave him a three-month sentence and took him to Lucknow jail. I came back to Delhi. The house was lying unattended and there was a child in my womb. My husband was jailed for three months. When he came back I was delivered of a boy. He had been given three hundred and fifty rupees by the army which we spent on the baby, but he died.

Afterwards, the same story started all over again. Drinking, beating, filthy abuses, suspicions. He would say "Why does this man come, why does that one come?" I'd answer, "I have given up everyone for you. I have given you my all, don't accuse me falsely." He'd pick up sticks, take out knives, and I would keep silent out of fear.

Then I gave birth to four daughters, one after another. After the fourth daughter he did not even let me rest. The third day after I gave birth he sent me to work in the kitchen. He had not let anyone from my family come and help me at the time of delivery. When the fifth child was about to come I said, "God, give me a son otherwise this man won't let me live." But those whose habits are bad do not change even if they have ten sons!

Gradually, we built a small house in Mehrauli and shifted there with our five daughters. I thought perhaps being among good people he might change. We also kept our hut in Madangir. But his habits worsened. He would beat me and tell me to get out of the house. But I thought of the future of my daughters, of their marriages. If I left the house, people would say I was a bad woman who has run off with a lover. There was a woman who lived next to us in Mehrauli. She did some black magic which made my eldest daughter very sick. I went to all the hospitals. Then someone sent me to the *baba* (holy man) of the Mehrauli tomb. Baba asked me not to worry and gave me some water in a bottle. The water cured my daughter. Baba also intimated that the neighboring woman had been responsible for the illness. So I asked my husband not to visit her. She turned him completely against me. She would make him drink and tell him that in his absence other men visited me.

One night, coming home drunk, he really wanted to kill me. With the children in tow I climbed up the rear wall and hid in a neighbor's house while he was out in the street looking for us with a drawn knife. We ran barefoot through the jungle at night and came to my sister's house. In the morning I went to the police station and got them to write down that I have left with my five daughters and nothing else so that he does not accuse me of theft. The next day I sent word to him through my sister's daughter. He told her in front of everyone that I should send our daughters out on the street, earn money by making them whores. I went to Eros Cinema, where he worked and asked him why he was making such a spectacle out of his family. He started beating me in front of a big crowd till my body was blue with bruises. But I did not fall down. When some taxi drivers intervened to save me, he ran away. We came back to Madangir and I started working. He would turn up every other day and abuse all of us "Sister-fuckers, whores, bastards, even prostitutes are better than you. Go and do your work in the streets." He called me such filthy names that I wished the earth would split open and take me in. After three months we all returned to Mehrauli.

Someone stole a lot of money from the cinema theater where he worked. He was also implicated in the theft, lost his job, and was arrested. I spent all my money running from one court to another, hiring a lawyer, finding the jail he was in and arranging bail. When they released him all he said was "Bitch, why did you spend all that money?"

My brother, my sister, and her children came to visit us. I cried a lot that day for my own sister betrayed me. I cannot bear to tell you. When a man becomes bad, women take advantage of him. First they asked me to cook for them and then I served them liquor. I also drank some but then went to sleep. Only heaven knows what he did that night. Three bottles of liquor had been consumed. My daughter woke up in the night and she saw my husband and my sister doing the work that is done between man and woman. My whole body trembled. I said to myself. "Now my house is ruined."

I told my mother. She is a frank woman and cannot tolerate any harm done to me. She went to my sister's house. "Why are you destroying that poor woman's home?" she said to her. When my sister discovered that I knew, she came to meet me. I did not say anything. I did not want to create a scene in front of the whole world. My sister only said, "Brother-in-law gave me some *roti* to eat and exacted its price."

Look, when a man is drunk, he does not distinguish between his wife, sister or even mother. He will fuck even his mother. When he came home in the evening I abused him roundly. I said "She may be my sister, she may be anyone. But if that woman crosses the threshold of my house, I will set her on fire and also burn myself."

One day he called me for "business" and when I took off my clothes, he said, "You can now get out of the house." I felt so humiliated. If I had had a tin of kerosene in front of me that night, I would have set myself on fire.

Look, there is one kind of love which makes the woman blind and lose her senses. There is another kind of love which is true and yet another which is false. A woman understands everything about the differences in the kinds of love. The woman may not speak but she understands. True love has a lot of *rasa* (literally "juice," "flavor"). False love is dry. The third one makes the woman blind so that she does not ask which other woman her man visits. These are the three kinds of love. He used to call me to bed once in ten or fifteen days only to make me blind.

Look, I didn't want him to feel any lack in love. If he called me twenty times, I went to him twenty times. If he called me ten times, I went ten times. A man goes out of the house only if he is not getting enough. So I never let him remain hungry. In the early days of the marriage he used to call me two to four times a day.

I drink sometimes. Liquor intoxicates in many ways. I am talking about myself. When a woman drinks she needs a man. Every woman will say that. She wants new men. It is natural to feel that way. My husband had no idea of intercourse in the beginning. He didn't even know about a woman's monthly periods. I taught him everything. I had such strength that even if he called me to bed twenty times it was too little for me. Now he has ruined my body. When I walked people used to say, "There comes the police inspector!" But the strength is gone now. Well, the strength is still there and will come out if he does not abuse me and shares his life with me. If he'd still love me I would forget everything. Earlier he used to call me "wrestler" and then he called me "head woman." Now it has come down to "bitch," "whore," and "*badmash*" (bad character). Once when he came home early and I was not there, for I had to attend a program of religious singing in our alley, he took out two tins of kerosene and said, "Before burning yourself arrange to have the news brought to me in the Cinema. I will come to throw your corpse away."

Then one day he went to work and met with an accident on the way. My sister's son brought him back, all bandaged and stitched. When I saw him I forgot all the woe he had caused me. My heart ached for him. I had eaten his salt and was true to him. When I brought him milk, he said, "Sister-fucker, go and give the milk to your parents to drink." Still in bandages, he went to work the next day and brought back papers for divorce. He told me to sign them. I said "First get well and then get the divorce." The children and I came back to Madangir. He stayed away for twelve days and then came home.

None of my wishes have been fulfilled. Before marriage I thought I will wear nice clothes and jewels and most of all that I will get love. I thought if our two hearts met and became one we could cross the span of this life together. For the first few years I kept the *vrata* of *karwa-chauth* (a day of fasting by married women for the welfare of their husbands). He said, "Why are you making this show? Why are you playing a role in a drama?" I said, "I have true love for you in my heart." How he has made me suffer!

They say there was once a bad man. People asked him why good men die but the bad ones don't. He replied that God doesn't take bad men because He knows that in heaven too the bad men will bring their filth in. See, Sita also suffered under great cruelties but she passed her time on earth for the love of one man. I too tolerated everything because I loved him. I couldn't live without him even if he abused me thousands of times. But a man who abuses and beats you in public, why should I love him? Now my love is slowly dying from inside. I only think of the children. He doesn't even know in which class the children are studying or whether they even go to school. In fact he now has his eyes on our third daughter who has just turned fourteen and I have to watch him carefully.

My health has been affected and my heart is affected. Sometimes I become mad. If a woman can talk then she remains sane, otherwise there is something inside her which keeps on pressing. By talking one can take the pressure out. I often talk to myself or start talking in front of children in the alley. Once in a while my children call me mad. In spite of all this I don't get angry. The children say, "Mother, you are made of stone." Despite saying all the filthy things to me over the years, he too has been defeated. But I have no anger. If he can get women from outside, we can also get other men. But to do so goes against my *dharma* and when I die only my *dharma* will go with me. They say that the man who spits on the sun gets the spit back on his own face. So he is the one whose face will be smeared with spittle. The love of a man and a woman is very strange. No one can give woman the love which a man can. A woman who loves a man from inside is hungry only for him. Now I would like to renounce the world and go away to a forest. I have hopes in my children but perhaps like my mother no one will care for me. It would have been better if I had married a blind man. At least I could have served him, been rewarded for performing good deeds. What did I get marrying someone with eyes—ruin, filth, and abuse.

Basanti

Before marriage, I lived happily with my parents in our village in Bihar. We were three brothers and three sisters. A brother was the eldest and I was the next in line. Two brothers and a sister are still unmarried.

I got along well with my parents but I loved my father best. I did all his work. Mother used to beat me. The whole day she abused me because I did not work and was busy playing. Two or three times a week I would get beaten by her. Because a mother teaches you to work, she also hits you more. I don't remember my childhood much except that I was happy, laughing even after being abused. We all loved each other but didn't talk much. I remember the festivals we celebrated. On *holi* (the spring festival of colors) we worshipped liquor. We made liquor from rice then put it in a brass dish with some *sal* leaves, worshipped it and then drank it. We also worshipped a chicken. We take out its blood and drink one drop. Everyone fasted for two to three days and then ate and drank. Then there was the worship of Kali (the fierce mother goddess) every year. Two days we fasted and the goddess would enter one of the women. While the goddess was in her no one went near her, not even her own children. Afterwards, we would go to the temple, offer milk, water and flowers for her worship and then bathe. But ever since I am here in Delhi I have left all the rituals because I took the wrong path. Every year we also went to see the play about Rama and Sita though I did not understand it much. Now I go to see it only because of the children.

When I became mature my parents married me off at fifteen. After marriage I went to live in Calcutta with my husband. We spent a very happy six years. I stayed at home while he worked. My husband treated me well and we did not lack anything. He talked lovingly to me and we laughed a lot. Twice a night we did "work." In the beginning it was very painful, but then I liked it. We slept apart only at the times of my period. At those times he would not even take water from my hands. Before sleeping we would drink, chew *pan* (betel leaf) and smoke cigarettes.

I was young in years and perhaps that is why I could not conceive. When the body is ready, the child too comes. After a while, I fell sick. There were dizzy spells, bouts of fever, and I became as thin as a stick. I couldn't even walk and my hearing was affected. I went to the doctor, daily drank coconut water for four months, and didn't eat. Perhaps Calcutta's water did not suit me. But because we were both so happy, even the fact that I couldn't conceive did not bother us. I thought, we two beings are together in a foreign land and when I get well we will go back to the village and perhaps it will happen there.

After returning to the village, I was quite unhappy. We sold our fields. He earned money by working as a laborer, and I supplemented the income by making and selling rice liquor. When I did not get a child he said there was no point in his keeping me. I said to him, "Only God can help us. If we don't have a child what can I do? Let's wait another four, five years." He started talking like this seven years after the marriage. When my sister-in-law came to visit us she said, "Why are you sad? When God is ready to give you a child, he will do so." I said, "But your brother has to understand this. Otherwise how will I live in his house?" Then my husband together with my mother-in-law stopped giving me food. I would also be beaten. My body became black and blue, with swellings and scars all over it. My husband would kick me and hit me with a stick.

He then said to me, "If you want to stay in my house you can do so, but only if you get me married for a second time." I said, "I will get you married but then I won't stay here. I will only get unhappiness. When you beat me so much now how can you treat me well after your second marriage?" He said he would keep his word. "You can live here in comfort and I will marry again." I gave him five hundred rupees of my own, three dresses and got him married. Though we all lived together for two years I was not happy. My husband slept between the two of us. Sometimes he would love one woman and sometimes the other.

One day he said, "Leave the house. I don't want to keep you." I walked off to commit suicide by throwing myself under a train. A boy from the village stopped me and said, "Why do you want to die? You are still young and all your limbs are strong and healthy. Why die?" I said, "I have no one now in this world. So why should I live?" When my husband heard about this he came immediately. I was sitting under a tree and he asked me to come home. I said "You drink liquor every day, you beat me. I won't go back with you." The other wife said, "Elder sister, if you won't stay then I will also leave the house. I will go anywhere, go away with any man, beg for my food but you should not leave. I would be very unhappy if you left."

My mother-in-law was a very bad woman. She would hit and kick me. She'd snatch away bread from me. When my man gave me a *roti* she would say, "Why are you giving her food? Don't give her anything to eat." When a person gets very unhappy only then does she leave her home. I was dejected that I was not conceiving and my man was also unhappy because of this, so I decided to go away. But before leaving, I broke everything in the house in my anger. I destroyed everything. I said "You want to destroy my home. So there! I will do it myself!" Before leaving I did not even take the three thousand rupees I had saved up. The other wife found it in the rice storage bin after I left. Afterwards, my husband would admiringly say to others, "How did she save so much money though we had so little!" He also said of me that she is very wise and he cannot understand why I broke everything and ran away.

Then my parents said, "You shouldn't worry. Earn for yourself. Take it easy and go wherever fate takes you. Go to the festivals, go to see the dances." But when the *jodi* (pair) is broken, how can one be happy! I was constantly with the women in the household and traded in rice like a merchant. Then I thought, "What happiness do I get in my parent's home?" When the brothers marry and bring their wives they might not want to keep me any longer! I told my father, "While you are alive I will work and use up all my strength. But when you die I will be feeble and no one will look after me. If I had a son or a daughter it might have been all right, but otherwise there will be no one to ask about my welfare." So I decided to come to Delhi because two of my brothers and a sister were already in this city. I came with a group of 30 to 40 men and women who were coming to work on construction sites. My father put me on the train.

After reaching Delhi I stayed with my brothers and sister in Sultanpur and began to work as a sweeper. There I met my second husband, who was a contractor and who gave my father fifteen hundred rupees to marry me. After marriage, Mannu's father (the second husband) said, "I have made a mistake in getting married. But don't be afraid, I will look after your needs till the end." His wife had died six years ago and he had children. Because his children objected, he told me to stay separately by myself. I said, "Fine, but you should keep on meeting me sometimes." Now his children are grown up and even they come to visit me. I tell my husband, "Do whatever you like. Keep another wife. Just provide me with food." But now he doesn't give me anything.

I work and earn myself. I have three children, two boys and a girl. My sister's two children are also with me because she is dead. Sometimes my mind tells me to marry again. My brother-in-law says he will take his children away. I say, "Let them be with me. Listen to me, otherwise you will regret it. Earn here and feed them here." Now we are going to fight the case of my sister because she was murdered. I used to be visited by the Goddess but I passed Her on to my sister because it exhausted me. The Goddess has now gone into the murderer. When the Goddess used to come into me my whole body would tremble. Now I am often sick. To take care of the visits of the Goddess one has to do a lot of things like not touching dirty utensils, cleaning the hut immediately with cowdung and so on. I cannot serve her now. I have to earn my living. As long as I am alive I will earn, feed the children, and when there are difficulties we will see what happens.

At the time of marriage I had no worry. God had created a good pair from the two of us. No old people to interfere. But when I think of the mistake he made by turning me out I feel my heart collapsing. How well I lived! Now I live in a shanty. God knows what will happen though I have stopped believing in Him. I don't know whether I will be happy or unhappy; whether I will get happiness when the children grow up.

But for now they have to be sent to school.

There is no profit in getting married, no advantage at all. When the children grow up, at least they will say she has brought us up by working so hard. People and relatives tell me to marry, but I don't want to extend my hand to anyone anymore. I don't want to go anywhere. Wherever there is a place for me I will stay.

I sometimes think that Mannu's father is old and about to die. I also feel ashamed to be with him. Mannu's father also beat me once. He said, "You talk to other men." I said, "When someone asks about my welfare then I have to reply. And then you make me unhappy. If you kept me happy I would not talk to other men." He kept quiet. I don't say any of this to my brothers and sisters because his honor would be smirched. I tell them that we live well, eat, and drink. For three years he hasn't given me anything. Not even a rag. Only for the children did he once take out a hundred rupees. I said, "If these are your children get clothes for them." So he brought them some rotten stuff.

I often don't remember my earlier married life. I am quite alone. No fucker cares for me. I only think of the children and get some happiness from them. Or occasionally my family members come for a visit, and we laugh and joke together and I get some happiness that way. Relatives bring me peace.

I have thought of drowning myself, but then think of the children. Sometimes I cry inside myself. I don't want to quarrel with anyone but if someone says untrue things about me I get into a rage. Here when people say that I'm a whore, that when working in the bungalows I get fucked in the ass, then I get furious. Where do I have the time for all that stuff? I don't even have time to sit.

There is another thing which makes me angry. This is the matter of love. There is a man here who must have given me some kind of potion to drink, which has trapped me in his love. I thought of him as a brother but then he did the bad work with me. If he still loved me, it would have been fine. But he neither talks to me nor wants me to talk to anyone else. He doesn't even talk to the children anymore. I feel so unhappy, and even the heart can stop beating with so much pain.

He doesn't talk to me because of that milk(seller) woman. "If you have done that mistake with me then I will go with you," I say. I won't marry him, but I won't let him get away from me. He is scared so he doesn't come. For six years he kept me, but now he doesn't care anymore. My husband knows about it. He says I am a young woman and he doesn't mind. Earlier, my lover looked after me well. Whenever he needed me at night, he took me to his hut. The children also called him "papa." But now he says he'll watch me from afar and that I shouldn't joke around with other men. He would have had an affair with the milk woman but I came between them. I told him that if he'd so much as touched her, I'd skin him alive. One day I saw them together. I pulled him away and took out my sandal to hit him. I said, "We have been lovers for six years but I have never taken out my sandal to hit you. But today you must decide. Tell me what is your relationship with this woman, otherwise I will beat you. You have ruined my life and I shall not spare you."

There were four or five other men standing there. The milk woman called me a whore. Then she kept quiet and I too calmed down. But from inside I feel a great anger. When I fight with him I feel a little relieved, but what can I do? If my pair (*jodi*) had not broken up I wouldn't be in this situation. I have gone from one man to another and ended up by loving three men. Now I shall never love or marry again. I'll earn and bring up my children. My daughter is maturing and I have to arrange her marriage. I have to save money for that . . . . But love causes me sadness from within. They say when insects burn in the forest everyone can see, but when one's heart is burning no one comes to know of it. I cannot even go to the temple because I have taken the wrong path. In our area they didn't let women get on the wrong track. She may not talk unnecessarily even to her relatives. As long as she is unmarried she has some freedom, but after marriage she can only go with her husband. She may not talk to other men. I have come away from all that and so I am suffering.

The squalor of slum life, as the narratives of Janak and Basanti reveal, does nothing to dim the luminosity of their romantic longing. On the contrary, the abysmal material conditions and the struggle against poverty arouses their "sense of life according to love" to its fullest wakefulness. The dream of the transforming power of love, of what the woman might have been if she were well and truly loved, is tenaciously clung to amidst (and perhaps because of) all the suffering and pathos of her existence.

The central image of this dream is of the *jodi*, the pair. The pair, of course, exerts a universally powerful pull on human imagination. To adopt Dostoevsky's observation on the lover's vision, in the pair we may sometimes see the other, and ourselves, as God might have done so. In Janak and Basanti's fantasy of the pair, there are echoes of another universal myth: of the philandering husband, and the abandoned wife faithfully preserving the sanctity of the marriage bed. Its Indian versions have tales of Parvati's anger and jealousy as Shiva continues on a path of unremitting seduction; of Radha alternately wrathful and pining away in solitude while Krishna dallies with other *gopis* (cow herdesses). Indeed, Jungians will see in the women's yearning for containment in a couple a manifestation of the "pairing instinct" which they would ascribe to the feminine aspects of the soul.[4] The women's pain, rage, jealousy, vengefulness and despair are then aroused less by the fact of the man's infidelity than in his denying her fulfilment of the need for completion in the pair.

Freudians, on the other hand, would try to pinpoint individual, life-historical needs in the woman's (or the man's) fantasy of the couple. The partner, according to Freud's view of what he called "object choice," is a replacement for an earlier counterplayer from infancy—usually the father, mother, or a sibling—who will compensate for the loss, disillusionment, and pain experienced in the earlier wishful pairing. The partner in the couple may thus fulfill one or more of a variety of needs. He may provide nutrients for the woman's sense of the self through his "mirroring" of her, reflecting back with favor and with a confirming glow in his eyes all her acts of relationship. He may, on the other hand, be an incorporation of the idealized Other in whom the woman seeks to merge, hoping therein to find a way to build cohesiveness and strength into her own self. The man can also be needed as a container for all the despised and disavowed aspects of the self. He may thus be an incarnation of the woman's negative identity—of all she fears she might be (or become) but dares not acknowledge. Here the partner can either be the repository of the woman's unacceptable sexual or aggressive impulses, living out her "wickedness," which then allows her to keep her "goodness" and "purity" intact, or, he may take over the weaker part of her self; the woman can then afford to be strong and energetic as long as her hidden conviction that she is their opposite, finds an expression in the man's manifestation of weakness and passivity.

I have little doubt that one or another or many of the Jungian and Freudian motivations also go into the construction of Janak and Basanti's dream of the *jodi*. Yet besides universal archetypes and individual fantasies, I believe there is also a cultural image which comes through sharply in the woman's yearning for the couple. Iconically, this cultural image is represented by the *ardhanarishwara*—"the Lord that is half woman"—form of the God Shiva. Displaying the attributes of both the sexes, with the right side male and the left female, this form of the god shows his body merged with that of his consort,

Uma or Parvati.

The *ardhanarishwara* then represents the wished-for oneness of the divine couple rather than the twoness of mortal spouses. The husband is not simply a partner, however intimate, for that would still highlight his separate, bounded, individuality. Instead, the cultural ideal visualizes the *jodi* as a single two-person entity.

Perhaps the psychological concept that comes closest to representing the woman's ideal in marriage is what the psychoanalyst Heinz Kohut has called the "selfobject."[5] A seemingly odd apparition, a selfobject neither coincides with the contours of the self nor is unreservedly the other but leads a nomadic existence in the intermediate space between the two. According to Kohut, the selfobjects of early childhood, of which the parental caretakers are the foremost, constitute the stuff of the self through a process of "transmuting internalization." In adult life, they provide the self with its vital nutrients.

The *jodi*, then, is a "cultural selfobject"—making a Hindu invoke Sita Ram and not Sita *and* Ram—Radhakrishna and not Radha *and* Krishna—which connects the woman to the community of Indian women and thus helps to maintain the vitality and continuity of her identity. Despite the realities of life in the slums, of wife-beating husbands and reluctant lovers, of adulterous liaisons and consensual marriages, it is the contribution of this ideal to maintaining a sense of the self which helps us to understand the tenacity with which Janak and Basanti, as also women from other strata of Indian society, cling to the notion of the indissolubility of the couple. The persistence and importance of the *jodi* for the woman's sense of identity helps us comprehend better why many women, in spite of their economic independence, choose to suffer humiliation rather than leave an oppressive husband; why some women, in times of extreme marital stress and a burning rage toward the spouse, exercise the option of suicide rather than separation.

6

Gandhi and Women

Continuing my search for facets of the man-woman relationship in India, I turn to the autobiographical writings of one of the greatest men of the twentieth century. Although my task of psychoanalytic deconstruction, the activity of taking a text apart by bringing out its latent meanings, remains the same, Gandhi's fame and status as a culture hero makes this enterprise both easier and more difficult.

The task is easier in that the retrospective narrative enrichment engaged in by every autobiographer—who consciously or otherwise selects and orders details of his life so as to create a coherent and satisfying story, explaining and indeed justifying his present situation for the particular audience he has in mind—is capable of correction and modification through the accounts of other actors involved in the hero's epic.[1] The inconsistencies and the omission of vital details which may otherwise mar the symmetry of the hero's unconscious myth about himself, are easier to detect in case of a man like Gandhi who has attracted so much biographical attention, both contemporary and posthumous. I may, though, add here that Gandhi's autobiographical writings, *The Story of My Experiments with Truth* the foremost among them, are marked by a candor and honesty which, if not unique, are certainly rare in the annals of self-narration. In his quasi-mystical preoccupation with "truth," the blame for any distortions in the story of his self-revelation can be safely laid at the door of the narrator's unconscious purposes rather than ascribed to any deliberate efforts at omission or concealment.

The work of deconstruction is made more difficult as Gandhi is the foremost culture-hero of modern India. For an Indian child, the faces of Gandhi and other heroes like Nehru and Vivekananda are identical, with the masks crafted by the culture in order to provide ideals for emulation and identification. Every child in India has been exposed to stock narratives that celebrate their genius and greatness, the portraits utterly devoid of any normal human blemish such as envy, anger, lust, ordinariness, pettiness, or stupidity. The Indian analyst, also a child of his culture, is thus bound to have a special kind of "counter-transference" towards the culture-hero as a biographical subject. In other words, the analytic stance of respectful empathy combined with critical detachment, difficult enough to maintain in normal circumstances, becomes especially so in the case of a man like Gandhi. His image is apt to merge with other idealized figures from the biographer's own past, who were loved and admired yet secretly rebelled against. The analytic stance must then be charted out between contradictory hagiographic and pathographic impulses that seek constantly to buffet it.

For the analyst, the story of a man's relationship with women inevitably begins ("and also ends," sceptics would add) with his mother. Yet we know the mother-son dyad to be the most elusive of all human relationships. Located in the life space before the birth of language, the effort to recapture the truth of the dyad through words alone can give but teasing intimations of the hallucinatory intensity of a period when the mother, after giving the son life, also gave him the world. With some exceptions, like that of Nabokov, a mother cannot speak to her son through memory alone.[2] *Her* truth lies in the conjunction, indeed confabulation of imagination, symbols and reality through which she was earlier perceived and through which she may be later conjured, the latter being a rare artist's gift. For others, including Gandhi, the truth of the dyad we once built with our mothers is but fragmentarily glimpsed in various maternal proxies—from inanimate objects ("part" or "transitional" objects in analytic parlance) which a child endows with her vital spirit, to the women who will later attract and hold him. Like all mothers, Putlibai, whose favorite Gandhi was by virtue of his being the youngest child and whose special object of care and concern he remained because of his sickly constitution, is an abiding yet diffuse presence in her son's inner life, an intensely luminous being albeit lacking definition. We will discover her chimerical presence in Gandhi's relationships with various other women in whom she was temporarily reincarnated, his wife Kasturbai the foremost among them.

In his autobiography, written over a five-year period during his mid-fifties, Gandhi begins the account of his sexual preoccupations and struggles with his marriage at the age of thirteen. He had been betrothed to Kasturbai Nakanji, the daughter of a well-to-do merchant in his hometown of Porbandar, since they were both seven years old. Now, with the two children entering puberty, the families decided that the time for the nuptials had finally arrived.

In Kathiawar, on the west coast of India, the region where Gandhi grew up and where his father was the prime minister of a small princely state, such child marriages were the norm rather than the exception. Writing forty-three years after the event, Gandhi could still recall the details of the marriage festivities. His elder brother and a cousin were to be married at the same time in one big ceremony and young Mohandas was excited by the prospect of new clothes, sumptuous wedding feasts, and the evenings and nights full of music and dance. During the ceremony itself, whenever the couple was required to hold hands for a particular rite, Mohandas would secretly give Kasturbai's hand a squeeze which she, in turn, eagerly reciprocated.

The excitement of the wedding was marred by one jarring incident. On his way to the celebrations, Mohandas's father had a serious accident when the horse-carriage he was traveling in overturned, and he arrived late for the ceremony, with bandages covering his arms and back. The young boy was much too excited by what was happening to him to pay attention to the injured father, a fact that the older man notes with shame. "I was devoted to my father but I was equally devoted to sensuality. Here by sensuality I do not mean one organ but the whole realm of sensual enjoyment."[3]

Looking back at his younger self, Gandhi feels that sex became an obsession with the adolescent Mohandas. At school, his thoughts were constantly with his wife, as he impatiently waited for the night to descend when he could go to her. He was also consumed by a raging jealousy. He wanted to know of every move his wife made in his absence and would forbid her to go out alone to the temple, on household errands or to meet girlfriends. Kasturbai was not the sort of girl to accept such unreasonable restrictions and accusations based on unfounded jealousy with any degree of equanimity. Small in stature, she was an attractive girl with glossy black hair, large dark eyes set deep in an oval face, a well-formed mouth, and a determined chin. She was by no means a female creature subservient to male whims and could easily be self-willed and impatient with her young husband. They had violent quarrels, dissolved in the love-making of the night, only to reemerge with the light of day.

Later in life, Gandhi, regretting his treatment of Kasturbai during the first fifteen years of their married life, gave two causes for his jealousy. The first was the projection of his own turbulent sexual wishes and fantasies onto his wife—"I took out my anger at her for my own weakness"—while the second was the influence of Sheikh Mehtab, the intimate friend of his youth. Physically strong, fearless, and rakishly handsome, while Mohandas was none of these, Sheikh Mehtab has been portrayed by Gandhi as his evil genius, the tempter whose blandishments Mohandas was incapable of resisting. The breacher of taboos and values Mohandas held dear, Sheikh Mehtab introduced the vegetarian lad to the guilt-ridden pleasures of eating meat, and was the organizer of their joint visit to a brothel. Mehtab constantly fueled Gandhi's suspicions with regard to Kasturbai's fidelity. Reading about their youthful transgressions a hundred years later, to us Mehtab does not appear especially evil. He is neither more nor less than an average representative of the world of male adolescence, with its phallic displays and the ethic of a devil-may-care bravery. For a thirteen-year-old (and from all accounts, including his own) "mama's boy," dealing with the sexual upsurge of adolescence at the same time as the demand for establishing an emotional intimacy with a strange girl, Sheikh Mehtab must have been a godsend. He provided Mohandas with the adolescent haven where young men can be both dismissive and fearful of women and heterosexual love, where in the vague homoeroticism of masculine banter and ceaseless activity a youth can gradually come to terms with the femininity within and without him. Little wonder that, in spite of the family's strong disapproval and Mohandas's own conscious view of their relationship as one between a reformer and a rake, their friendship remained close and lasted for almost twenty years. During his sojourn in England Gandhi sent Mehtab money from his meagre allowance, voluntarily sought him out again after his return to India and later took his friend with him when he sailed for South Africa.

Two circumstances, Gandhi writes, saved him from becoming an emotional and physical wreck during the initial phase of his marriage. The first was the custom among the Hindus, wisely aware of the consuming nature of adolescent passion, of separating the husband and wife for long periods during the first years of marriage. Kasturbai was often away on extended visits to her family and Gandhi estimates that in the first six years of their married life they could not have lived together for more than half of this period.

The second saving circumstance was Gandhi's highly developed sense of duty, both as a member of a large extended family, with an assigned role and definite tasks, and as a son who was especially conscientious and conscious of his obligation to an ageing and ailing father. After coming home from school, Gandhi would first spend time with his father, massaging his legs and attending to his other needs. Even when he was thus engaged, his mind wandered as he impatiently waited for the filial service to come to an end, his fantasies absorbed by the images of his girl-wife in another room of the house. As all readers of his autobiography know, the conflict between sexual desire and his sense of duty and devotion to the father was to load the marriage, especially its physical side, with an enormous burden of guilt. We shall briefly recapitulate the incident that has often been reproduced either as a cautionary moral tale or as a choice text for psychoanalytical exegesis.

Gandhi's father had been seriously ill and his younger brother had come to look after him, a task he shared with the son. One night around ten-thirty or eleven, while Gandhi was massaging his father's legs, his uncle told him to rest. Happily, Gandhi rushed off to the bedroom to wake up his pregnant wife for sexual intercourse. After a few minutes, a servant knocked at the bedroom door and informed the couple that the father had expired. Gandhi talks of his life-long feeling of remorse that blind lust had deprived him of the chance of rendering some last service to his father and thus missing the patriarch's "blessing" which was instead received by the uncle. "This is the shame I hinted at in the last chapter," he writes,

> my sexual obsession even at the time of service to my father. Till today I have not been able to wash away this dark stain. I cannot forget that though my devotion to my parents was boundless and I could have given up every-thing for them, my mind was not free of lust even at that critical moment. This was an unforgivable lack in my service to my father. This is why in spite of my faithfulness to one woman I have viewed myself as someone blinded by sexuality. It took me a long time to free myself of lust and I have had to undergo many ordeals before I could attain this freedom.
>
> Before I close this chapter of my double shame I also want to say that the child born to my wife did not survive for more than a couple of days. What other outcome could there have been?[4]

Sexual passion endangers all the generations, Gandhi seems to say, not only the parents to whom one is morally and filially obliged, but the children conceived in sexual union.

At the age of eighteen, Mohandas left his wife and family behind (a son had been recently born) as he sailed for England to study law. He faced a good deal of opposition to his plans from his family and his community, which propounded the orthodox view that a man could not remain a good Hindu if he went abroad. Gandhi could leave for England with his family's consent (the community was not so easily mollified and declared him an outcaste) only after he made a solemn vow to his mother to avoid scrupulously the three inflamers of passion, "wine, women, and meat"—the anxious Hindu counterpart of the more cheerful "wine, women, and song"—during his sojourn in that distant island.

Gandhi's account of his three-year stay in England is striking in many ways. V. S. Naipaul has pointed out Gandhi's intense self-absorption, which made him oblivious to all the externals of his surroundings.[5] Gandhi does not mention the climate or the seasons. He does not describe London's buildings and streets, nor touch upon its social, intellectual, and political life.

What he immerses himself in and passionately discovers are fringe groups and causes which the mainstream English society would have unhesitatingly labeled "eccentric." An active member of the London Vegetarian Society and the "Esoteric Christian Union" (many years later in South Africa he would proudly identify himself as the agent for these Societies on his letterhead), he was also a fervent admirer of Annie Besant, the heir of the Russian mystic Madame Blavatsky, and a self-declared "bride of Christ."

Knowing that till very recently (and again in the future) the core of Gandhi's self-absorption was his concern with his sexuality, the meager space he devotes to the stirring of sexual desire is even more striking. In the full flush of youth, learning such English graces as dancing, and becoming somewhat of a dandy, this passionate young man—a (however reluctant) sensualist—tells us very little about how he dealt with his desires and their inevitable stimulation in a society where the sexes mingled much more freely than in his native Kathiawar. The only exception to this silence is an incident near the end of his stay, when Gandhi was attending a conference of vegetarians in Portsmouth and stayed with a friend at the house of a woman, "not a prostitute but of easy virtue." At night, while the three of them were playing cards, there was much sexual banter in which Gandhi enthusiastically participated. Gandhi was ready, as he says, "to descend from speech into action," when his friend reminded him of his vows.

> I was embarrassed. I came to my senses. In my heart I was
> grateful to the friend. I remembered my vow to my mother.
> I was trembling when I reached my room. My heart was
> racing. My condition was that of a wild animal who has just

escaped the hunter. I think this was the first occasion I was
"possessed by passion" for a woman not my wife and
desired to "make merry" with her.[6]

This is the only explicit event in which higher duty opposed and
conquered sexual temptation that is reported in this part of Gandhi's
autobiography. The earlier sexual preoccupation, I would surmise,
went underground, to reemerge in two different streams which on the
surface seem quite unrelated to genital sexuality. One of these streams
is Gandhi's increasing preoccupation with religious and spiritual
matters. He tells us of his visits to theosophists, conversations with
Christian clergymen, the reading of inspirational and religious literature. At times, Gandhi seems to be quite aware of the connection
between his sexual struggles and his spiritual interests. Thus he notes
down the following verses from the *Bhagavad Gita* :

If one
Ponders on objects of the senses there springs
Attraction; from attraction grows desire,
Desire flames to fierce passion, passion breeds
Recklessness; then the memory—all betrayed—
Lets noble purpose go, and saps the mind,
Till purpose, mind, and man are all undone.

"These verses," he says, "made a deep impression on my mind, and they
still ring in my ears."[7]

The other stream is his obsession with food, an obsession that was
to remain with him for the rest of his life. Page after page, in dreary
detail, we read about what Gandhi ate and what he did not, why he
partook of certain foods and why he did not eat others, what one eminent
vegetarian told him about eggs and what another, equally eminent,
denied. The connection between sexuality and food is made quite
explicit in Gandhi's later life when his ruminations about his celibacy
would almost invariably be followed by an exhaustive discussion of the
types of food that stimulate desire and others that dampen it. Again, we
must remember that in the Indian consciousness, the symbolism of food
is more closely or manifestly connected to sexuality than it is in the
West. The words for eating and sexual enjoyment, as A. K. Ramanujan
reminds us, have the same root, *bhuj*, in Sanskrit, and sexual intercourse
is often spoken about as the mutual feeding of male and female.[8]

On his return to India, Gandhi was faced with the necessity of making a living as a lawyer, a task for which he found himself both professionally and personally ill-equipped. A section of his caste was still hostile to him, having never forgiven him for his defiance of its mandate not to go abroad. There were further difficulties in his adjustments to the norms and mores of life in an Indian extended family—and in the family's adjustments to the newly acquired habits and values of its somewhat anglicized member. Today, with infinitely larger numbers of people moving across cultural boundaries and back again, the urbane Indian might indulgently smile at the tragicomic aspects of this reverse cultural shock. Tea and coffee, oatmeal porridge and cocoa were introduced to the breakfast table of the Gandhi household. Boots, shoes—and smelly socks—were to be worn in the burning heat of Kathiawar. Indeed, as a colonial subject, his identification with the British overlord was so strong that when some years later he was to sail for South Africa, he insisted on his sons being dressed like English public school boys with Etonian collars and ties. Poor Kasturbai was to dress up as a British lady—corset, bustle, high lace collar, laced shoes, and all. Her vehement protests and perhaps the absurdity of it all made him finally relent, though Kasturbai still had to dress up as a Parsi lady, a member of the community most respected by the British.

The marriage was still tempestuous, his driven genital desire the cause of these storms. His stay in England had neither reduced the strength of Gandhi's jealousy nor put an end to the nagging suspicions about his wife's fidelity. At the egging on of his old friend Sheikh Mehtab, Gandhi went so far as to break Kasturbai's bangles—to an Indian girl the dreaded symbol of widowhood—and to send her back to her parents' house. It took him a year before he consented to receive her back and over four years before his suspicion was stilled.[9] Purists can be cruel, especially to those dependent women who threaten to devour their virtue.

Economic, social, and familial conflicts, besides the perennial erotic one, seem to have spurred Gandhi's travels on the spiritual path. In this journey he now acquired a guide, Raichandra, a young jeweler. Raichandra was a man after Gandhi's own heart, more interested in *moksha* (the release from the cycles of birth and death which Hindus believe govern the wandering of the individual soul) than in diamonds. The two men met often to discuss spiritual topics and the depth of Raichandra's sincerity, purpose, and knowledge of Hindu thought and scriptures made a deep impression on Gandhi's mind. Of the three men, he says, who had the greatest influence on his life (the others were Tolstoy and Ruskin), Raichandra was the only one with whom he had a long personal association. Indeed, the young jeweler who talked so eloquently about *moksha* was the nearest Gandhi came to having a guru, and "In my moments of inner crisis, it was Raichandra with whom I used to seek refuge."[10]

Unfortunately, in spite of the vast amount written on his life (over four hundred biographical items), and the wealth of material contained in the ninety volumes of Gandhi's collected works, we know very little of the subjects of these talks, the letters they exchanged, or the kind of guidance Gandhi sought for his inner turbulence. From the available references, scattered in Gandhi's writings, it is evident that a central concern of their earnest exchanges was the relationship of sexuality to "salvation," the transformation of sexual potency into psychic and spiritual power—the core issue, in fact, of much of Hindu metaphysics and practice. Gandhi notes that the idea that "milk gives birth to sexual passions is something which I first learnt from Raichandrabhai," and he ascribes to the jeweler the predominant role in his decision to become a celibate.[11]

In 1893, at the age of twenty-four, Gandhi left for South Africa where he had been engaged as a lawyer by an Indian businessman. With brief interruptions for home visits, he was to stay there for the next twenty-two years.

Gandhi's years in South Africa, especially from 1900 to 1910, roughly spanning the fourth decade of his life, were crucial for the formation of Gandhi's historical persona. During these years Gandhi remade himself in that final image which is now evoked by his name. The first great nonviolent political campaigns for the rights of Indians living in South Africa, which introduced and refined the instrument of *Satyagraha* (literally, insistence on truth), took place during this period at the end of which he would become well-known in many parts of the world. Equally important for our purposes is the fact that it was also during these years that he defined for himself the kind of personal life he would lead and developed his ideas on the desired relationship between the sexes which would form the foundation for his own marriage with Kasturbai.

Founding and living in communes with disciples and seekers who shared his vision, radically experimenting with food and alternative systems of healing such as nature cure, generally embracing an ascetic lifestyle, the cornerstone of his personal life was *brahmacharya* or celibacy. Indeed *brahmacharya* was one leg of a tripod of which the other two were nonviolence (*ahimsa*) and truth (*satya*), which he adopted as the conscious basis for his adult identity and about which he would later write: "Nonviolence came to me after a strenuous struggle, *brahmacharya* I am still struggling for, but truth has always come naturally to me."[12]

The decision for sexual abstinence was taken in 1901, the year in which Raichandra died and in which Gandhi had just become a father for the fourth time (Devdas, the youngest son, was born in 1900). Both these circumstances must have contributed to Gandhi's resolve to renounce sexuality. The birth of the son, as we know from the account of the fateful night of the father's death and the newborn who did not survive because of *his father's* accursed lust, was a reminder of Gandhi's despised genital desires and therefore a stigma. To give them up was an offering made at the altar of Raichandra's (and, we would conjecture, his father's) departed soul. Kasturbai had not been consulted and Gandhi confesses that for the first few years he was only "more or less successful" in his practice of self-restraint.[13] Gandhi had left for India with his family in November 1901 and returned to South Africa the next year after promising his wife that she would soon follow. Yet once he was back in South Africa, Gandhi was reluctant to have Kasturbai join him. Paramount in his decision must have been the fact that his resolve to abstain from sexual intercourse was still fragile. The monetary argument he advances in the letters to his relatives, where he asks their help in persuading his wife to remain behind for two to three years, namely, that the savings he could make in South Africa would enable her and the children to lead an easy life in India,[14] neither jibes with the realities of running a household alone nor with Gandhi's character and temperament. Only a few months earlier, while leaving for India, he had gifted all the gold and diamond jewelery presented to him by a grateful Indian community to a trust, maintaining, "I feel neither I nor my family can make any personal use of the costly present," and that what he valued was their affection and not money.[15]

Gandhi finally took the vow to observe complete celibacy in 1906 when he was thirty-seven years old, on the eve of his first nonviolent political campaign in South Africa. The preceding five years of attempted abstinence he felt, had only been a preparation for what would amount to a total and irrevocable renunciation of sexuality. The example of Tolstoy further deepened his resolve. As he writes in 1905, "He (Tolstoy) used to enjoy all pleasures of the world, kept mistresses, drank and was strongly addicted to smoking. . . . He has given up all his vices, eats very simple food and has it in him no longer to hurt any living creature by thought, word or deed."[16] Tolstoy's ideas on chastity, not only for the unmarried but also for the married, outlined in the *Kreuzer Sonata* (1889), were combined with the Hindu notions on *brahmacharya* to form Gandhi's own vision of the "right" relationship between men and women. More than a personal code of conduct, these ideas regulated the life of all those who lived with him in his various communes (*ashrams*) in South Africa and India. Briefly summarized in his own words, this doctrine on the relationship between a couple holds that

> The very purpose of marriage is restraint and sublimation of the sexual passion. Marriage for the satisfaction of sexual appetite is *vyabhichara*, concupiscence. . . if they come together merely to have a fond embrace they are nearest the devil.
>
> The only rule that can be laid down in such instances (if a child is not conceived) is that coitus may be permitted once at the end of the monthly period till conception is established. If its object is achieved it must be abjured forthwith.
>
> There is no doubt that much of the sensuality of our nature, whether male or female, is due to the superstition, having a religious sanction, that married people are bound to share the same bed and the same room. But every husband and wife can make a fixed resolution from today never to share the same room or same bed at night, and to avoid sexual contact, except for one supreme purpose which it is intended for in both man and beast.[17]

Whatever its other consequences, there is little doubt that Gandhi's vow of celibacy distinctly improved his marriage, perhaps because poor Kasturbai was no longer perceived as a seductive siren responsible for his lapses from a longed-for ideal of purity. Ever since they had been in South Africa, there was much bickering and quarreling between the two. They had fought over her desire to keep her ornaments while Gandhi sought to convince her of the virtues of nonpossession. There was a major explosion, in which Gandhi almost turned her out of the house, over his wish that she clean up after an untouchable Christian visitor, a task abhorrent to a traditional Hindu woman with her deeply ingrained taboos about pollution. There was a running battle between the couple over their eldest son Harilal's wish that he grow up like other boys of his age and be allowed to avail of formal schooling. Gandhi's radical views on education would not allow the son to be sent to school, while Kasturbai was obstinate in the advocacy of her firstborn's cause.

From all accounts, before the vow of *brahmacharya*, Gandhi was an autocrat with his wife, "completely steel," as he tried to bend her to his will and get her to embrace what must have appeared to her as eccentric notions that endangered the present and future welfare of the family.

After 1906, their relationship improved steadily and Gandhi could write with some justification that "I could not steal into my wife's heart until I decided to treat her differently than I used to do, and so I restored to her all her rights by dispossessing myself of any so-called rights as her husband."[18] In their later years, though there were occasional disagreements, generally with respect to the children and Kasturbai's discomfort with the many women in the various *ashrams* who jostled each other to come closer to Gandhi, the marriage was marked by deep intimacy and a quiet love which impressed everyone who witnessed the old couple together.

For Gandhi, celibacy was not only the sine qua non for *moksha*, but also the mainspring of his political activities. It is from the repudiation, the ashes of sexual desire, that the weapon of nonviolence which he used so effectively in his political struggle against the racial oppression of the South African white rulers and later against the British empire, was phoenix-like born. As Gandhi puts it :

> *Ahimsa* (nonviolence) means Universal Love. If a man gives his love to one woman, or a woman to one man, what is there left for the world besides? It simply means, "We two first, and the devil take all the rest of them." As a faithful wife must be prepared to sacrifice her all for the sake of her husband, and a faithful husband for the sake of his wife, it is clear that such persons cannot rise to the height of Universal Love, or look upon all mankind as kith and kin. For they have created a boundary wall round their love. The larger their family, the farther are they from Universal Love. Hence one who would obey the law of *ahimsa* cannot marry, not to speak of gratification outside the marital bond.[19]

As for those who are already married,

If the married couple can think of each other as brother and sister, they are freed for universal service. The very thought that all women in the world are his sisters, mothers and daughters will at once enable a man to snap his chains.[20]

The truth of Gandhi's assertion that sexual love limits rather than expands personal concerns and that the narrow role of a husband is antithetical to the larger identity of one who would husband the world is not at issue here. Our intention for the moment is to elucidate Gandhi's conflict in the way he viewed it—in this case, the imperatives of desire straining against the higher purpose of unfettered service to community. Yet another of his pansexualist formulations of the conflict has it that the gratification of sexual passion vies with a man's obligation to enhance personal vitality and psychic power. "A man who is unchaste loses stamina, becomes emasculated and cowardly,"[21] is a sentiment often echoed in his writings as is the reiteration that his capacity to work in the political arena was a result of the psychic power gained through celibacy. Still another, later formulation is put in religious and spiritual terms—sexuality compromises his aspiration to become "God's eunuch." Reminiscent of Christ's metaphors of inno-cent childhood to describe would-be entrants to the kingdom of heaven and Prophet Mohammed's welcoming of "those made eunuchs," not through an operation but through prayer to God, Gandhi too would see sexual renunciation as a precondition for self-realization and, Moses-like, for seeing God "face to face."

Like his communes, which are a combination of the *ashrama* of the ancient sages described in the Hindu epics and the Trappist monastery in South Africa which so impressed him on a visit, Gandhi's views on the importance and merits of celibacy too seem to be derived from a mixture of Hindu and Christian religious traditions. Where Gandhi proceeded to give these views a special twist, going much beyond the cursory juxtaposition of sexuality and eating made in his culture, was in emphasizing, above all, the relation of food to the observance of celibacy. Experiments with food, to find that elusive right combination which would keep the libido effectively dammed, continued right through to the end of his life. In South Africa, as reported by an admiring yet detached disciple, there were months of cooking without salt or any condiments. Another period witnesses the absence of sugar, dates, and currants being added for sweetening purposes. This was followed by a period of "unfired" food served with olive oil. "Food values were most

97

earnestly discussed, and their effect upon the human body and its moral qualities solemnly examined. For a time a dish of raw chopped onions, as a blood purifier, regularly formed part of the dinner meal. . . . Ultimately Mr. Gandhi came to the conclusion that onions were bad for the passions, and so onions were cut out. Milk, too, Mr. Gandhi said, affected the 'passion' side of human life and thereafter milk was abjured likewise. 'We talk about food quite as much as gourmands do,' I said on one occasion to Mr. Gandhi. 'I am sure we talk about food more than most people; we seem to be always thinking of the things we either may or may not eat. Sometimes, I think it would be better if we just ate anything and did not think about it at all."[22] But for Gandhi food was a deathly serious business.

> Control of palate is very closely connected with the obser-
> vance of *brahmacharya* (celibacy). I have found from ex-
> perience that the observance of celibacy becomes compara-
> tively easy, if one acquires mastery over the palate. This
> does not figure among the observances of time-honoured
> recognition. Could it be because even great sages found it
> difficult to achieve. Food has to be taken as we take
> medicine, without thinking whether it is tasty or otherwise,
> and only in quantities limited to the needs of the body. . . .
> And one who thus gives up a multitude of eatables will
> acquire self-control in the natural course of things.[23]

The above passage is reminiscent of St. Augustine who, too, would take food as physic, strive daily against concupiscence in eating and drinking, and assert that "the bridle of the throat then is to be held attempered between slackness and stiffness."[24] St. Augustine's attitude toward food, though, is part of his attempt to gain a general freedom from the grip of sensuality, including "the delights of the ear (that) had more firmly entangled and subdued me."[25] Augustine treats imbibition as he does all sensory input. Gandhi, on the other hand, makes of food a primary regulator of the genital impulses. "A man of heightened sexual passion," he writes, "is also greedy of the palate. This was also my condition. To gain control over the organs of both generation and taste has been difficult for me."[26]

A radical cure for his epicurean disease is, of course, fasting, and Gandhi was its enthusiastic proponent. "As an external aid to *brahma-charya,* fasting is as necessary as selection and restriction of diet. So overpowering are the senses that they can be kept under control only when they are completely hedged in on all sides, from above and from beneath."[27] Remembering Gandhi's great fasts during his political struggles, we can see how fasting for him would have another, more personal meaning as a protector of his cherished celibacy and thus an assurance against the waning of psychic, and, with it, political power.

Battle, weapons, victory and defeat are a part of Gandhi's imagery in his account of a life-long conflict with the dark god of desire, the only opponent he did not engage nonviolently nor could ever completely subdue. The metaphors that pervade the descriptions of this passionate conflict are of "invasions by an insidious enemy" who needs to be implacably "repulsed"; while the perilous struggle is like "walking on a sword's edge." The god himself (though Gandhi would not have given Kama, the god of love, the exalted status accorded him in much of Hindu mythology) is the "serpent which I know will bite me," "the scorpion of passion," whose destruction, annihilation, conflagration, is a supreme aim of his spiritual strivings. In sharp contrast to all his other opponents, whose humanity he was always scrupulous to respect, the god of desire was the only antagonist with whom Gandhi could not compromise and whose humanity (not to speak of his divinity) he always denied.

For Gandhi, defeats in this war were occasions for bitter self-reproach and a public confession of his humiliation, while the victories were a matter of joy, "fresh beauty," and an increase in vigor and self-confidence that brought him nearer to the *moksha* he so longed for. Whatever may be his values to the contrary, a sympathetic reader, conscious of Gandhi's greatness and his prophetic insights into many of the dilemmas of modern existence, cannot fail to be moved by the dimensions of Gandhi's personal struggle—heroic in its proportion, startling in its intensity, interminable in its duration. By the time Gandhi concludes his autobiography with the words :

> To conquer the subtle passions seems to me to be far harder than the conquest of the world by the force of arms. Ever since my return to India I have had experiences of the passions hidden within me. They have made me feel ashamed though I have not lost courage. My experiments with truth have given, and continue to give, great joy. But I know that I must traverse a perilous path. I must reduce myself to zero,[28]

no reader can doubt his passionate sincerity and honesty. His is not the reflexive, indeed passionless moralism of the more ordinary religionist.

How did Gandhi himself experience sexual desire, the temptations and the limits of the flesh? To know this, it is important that we listen closely to Gandhi's voice describing his conflicts in the language in which he spoke of them—Gujarati, his mother tongue. Given the tendency toward hagiolatry among the followers of a great man, their translations, especially of the Master's sexual conflicts, are apt to distort the authentic voice of the man behind the saint. The English translation of Gandhi's autobiography by his faithful secretary, Mahadev Desai, in spite of the benefit of Gandhi's own revision, suffers seriously from this defect, and any interpretations based on this translation are in danger of missing Gandhi's own experience. Take, for instance, one famous incident from Gandhi's youth, of the schoolboy Gandhi visiting a prostitute for the first time in the company of his Muslim friend and constant tempter, Sheikh Mehtab. The original Gujarati version describes the incident as follows:

> I entered the house but he who is to be saved by God
> remains pure even if he wants to fall. I became almost blind
> in that room. I could not speak. Struck dumb by embarrass-
> ment, I sat down on the cot with the woman but could not
> utter a single word. The woman was furious, gave me a
> couple of choice abuses and showed me to the door [my
> translation].[29]

The English translation, however, is much less matter-of-fact. It is full of Augustinianisms in which young Gandhi goes into a "den of vice" and tarries in the "jaws of sin." These are absent in the original. By adding adjectives such as "evil" and "animal" before "passions," the translation seems to be judging them in a Christian theological sense that is missing in Gandhi's own account. St. Augustine, for instance—with whose *Confessions* Gandhi's *Experiments* has much in common—was rent asunder because of the "sin that dwelt in me," by "the punishment of a sin more freely committed, in that I was a son of Adam."[30] Gandhi, in contrast, uses two words, *vishaya* and *vikara*, for lust and passion respectively. The root of *vishaya* is from poison, and that is how he regards sexuality—as poisonous, for instance, when he talks of it in conjunction with serpents and scorpions. The literal meaning of *vikara*, or passion, is "distortion," and that is how passions are traditionally seen in the Hindu view, waves of mind that distort the clear waters of the soul. For Gandhi, then, lust is not sinful but poisonous, contaminating the elixir of immortality. It is dangerous in and of itself, "destructuralizing" in psychoanalytic language, rather than merely immoral, at odds, that is, with certain social or moral injunctions. To be passionate is not to fall from a state of grace, but to suffer a distortion of truth. In contrast to the English version, which turns his very Hindu conflict into a Christian one, Gandhi's struggle with sexuality is not essentially a conflict between sin and morality, but rather one between psychic death and immortality, on which the moral quandary is superimposed.

We can, of course, never be quite certain whether Gandhi was a man with a gigantic erotic temperament or merely the possessor of an overweening conscience that magnified each departure from an unattainable ideal of purity as a momentous lapse. Nor is it possible, for that matter, to evaluate the paradoxical impact of his scruples in intensifying the very desires they opposed. Both fueled each other, the lid of self-control compressing and heating up the contents of the cauldron of desire, in Freud's famous metaphor, their growing intensity requiring ever greater efforts at confinement.

Gandhi himself, speaking at the birth centenary of Tolstoy in 1928, warns us to refrain from judgments. While talking of the import of such struggles in the lives of great *homo religiosi*, he seems to be asking for empathy rather than facile categorization:

> The seeming contradictions in Tolstoy's life are no blot on
> him or sign of his failure. They signify the failure of the
> observer. . . . Only the man himself knows how much he
> struggles in the depth of his heart or what victories he wins
> in the war between Rama and Ravana.* The spectator
> certainly cannot know that.[31]

In judging a great man, Gandhi goes on to say, and here he seems to be talking as much of himself as Tolstoy,

> God is witness to the battles he may have fought in his
> heart and the victories he may have won. These are the only
> evidence of his failures and successes. . . . If anyone
> pointed out a weakness in Tolstoy though there could

*The good and evil protagonists of the Indian epic, *Ramayana*.

hardly be an occasion for anyone to do so for he was
pitiless in his self-examination, he would magnify that
weakness to fearful proportions. He would have seen his
lapse and atoned for it in the manner he thought most
appropriate before anyone had pointed it out to him.[32]

This is a warning we must take seriously but do not really need. Our
intention is not to "analyze" Gandhi's conflict in any reductionist sense
but to seek to understand it in all its passion—and obscurity. Gandhi's
agony is ours as well, after all, an inevitable by-product of the long
human journey from infancy to adulthood. We all wage wars on our
wants.

A passionate man who suffered his passions as poisonous of his
inner self and a sensualist who felt his sensuality distorted his inner
purpose, Gandhi's struggle with what he took to be the god of desire was
not unremitting. There were long periods in his adulthood when his
sensuality was integrated with the rest of his being. Old movie clips and
reminiscences of those who knew him in person attest to some of this
acceptable sensuality. It found expression in the vigorous grace of his
locomotion; the twinkle in his eye and the brilliance of his smile; the
attention he paid to his dress—even if the dress was a freshly laundered,
spotless loincloth; the care he directed to the preparation and eating of
his simple food; the delight with which he sang and listened to
devotional songs; and the pleasure he took in the daily oil massage of
his body. The Christian St. Augustine would have been altogether
shocked. Here, then, the Indian ascetic's path diverges from that trod by
the more austere and self-punishing Western monk. Here, too, from
Gandhi's sensuous gaiety, stems his ability to rivet masses of men not
by pronouncement in scripture but by his very presence.

In Gandhi's periods of despair, occasioned by real-life disappointments and setbacks in the sociopolitical campaigns to which he had
committed his life, the integration of his sensuality and spirituality
would be threatened and again we find him obsessively agonizing over
the problem of genital desire. Once more he struggled against the
reemergence of an old antagonist whom he sought to defeat by public
confessions of *his* defeats.

One such period spans the years between 1925 and 1928, after his
release from jail, when he was often depressed, believing that the Indian
religious and political divisions were too deep for the country to
respond to his leadership and that Indians were not yet ready for his kind
of nonviolent civil disobedience. There was a breakdown with a serious

condition of hypertension and doctors had advised him long rest. Interestingly, this is also the period in which he wrote his confessional autobiography, where he despondently confides, "Even when I am past fifty-six years, I realize how hard a thing it (celibacy) is. Every day I realize more and more that it is like walking on the sword's edge, and I can see every moment the necessity of continued vigilance."[33] His ideals and goals failing him, Gandhi finds sublime purpose and intent crumbling, exposing desires held in abeyance. These then become prepotent. The psychoanalyst would speak in this instance of the disintegration of "sublimations"—conversions of base wishes into socially sanctioned aspirations—and the lonely, painful regression which ensues.

In the copious correspondence of the years 1927 and 1928, the two longest and the most personally involved letters are neither addressed to his close political co-workers and leaders of future free India such as Nehru, Patel or Rajagopalachari, nor do they deal with vital political or social issues. The addressees are two unknown young men, and the subject of the letters is the convolutions of Gandhi's instinctual promptings. Responding to Balakrishna Bhave, who had expressed doubts about the propriety of Gandhi placing his hands on the shoulders of young girls while walking, Gandhi conducts a characteristic, obsessive search for any hidden eroticism in his action.[34] The other letter, to Harjivan Kotak, deserves to be quoted at some length since it details Gandhi's poignant struggle, his distress at the threatened breakdown of the psycho-sensual synthesis.

When the mind is disturbed by impure thoughts, instead of trying to drive them out one should occupy it in some work, that is, engage it in reading or in some bodily labor which requires mental attention too. Never let the eyes follow their inclination. If they fall on a woman, withdraw them immediately. It is scarcely necessary for anyone to look straight at a man's or woman's face. This is the reason why *brahmacharis*, and others too, are enjoined to walk with their eyes lowered. If we are sitting, we should keep them steady in one direction. This is an external remedy, but a most valuable one. You may undertake a fast if and when you find one necessary. . . . You should not be afraid even if you get involuntary discharges during a fast. *Vaids* (traditional doctors) say that, even when impure desires are absent, such discharges may occur because of pressure in

the bowels. But, instead of believing that, it helps us more
to believe that they occur because of impure desires. We
are not always conscious of such desires. I had involuntary
discharges twice during the last two weeks. I cannot recall
any dream. I never practised masturbation. One cause of
these discharges is of course my physical weakness but I
also know that there are impure desires deep down in me. I
am able to keep out such thoughts during waking hours.
But what is present in the body like some hidden poison,
always makes its way, even forcibly sometimes. I feel
unhappy about this, but am not nervously afraid. I am
always vigilant. I can suppress the enemy but have not been
able to expel him altogether. If I am truthful, I shall
succeed in doing that too. The enemy will not be able to
endure the power of truth. If you are in the same condition
as I am, learn from my experience. In its essence, desire for
sex-pleasure is equally impure, whether its object is one's
wife or some other woman. Its results differ. At the moment, we are thinking of the enemy in his essential nature.
Understand, therefore, that so far as one's wife is concerned you are not likely to find anyone as lustful as I was.
That is why I have described my pitiable condition to you
and tried to give you courage.[35]

A "hidden power," an "enemy to be expelled"—in such circumstances the body becomes a strange land inhabited by demons of feeling
and impulse divided from the self. With setbacks in a unity of intent,
there is a further fragmenting of the self. The moral dilemma stirs
conflicts of a primeval order, when early "introjects"—those presences
bound to desire out of which we construct our primary self—are
awakened, taste blood or better, poison, and threaten our identity—our
sense of wholeness, continuity, and sameness.

Another emotionally vulnerable period comprises roughly eighteen
months from the middle of 1935 onwards, when Gandhi was almost
sixty-six years old. Marked by a "nervous breakdown," when his blood
pressure went dangerously out of control, Gandhi was advised complete rest for some months by his doctors. He attributed this breakdown
to overwork and especially mental exhaustion brought on by the
intensity of his involvement and emotional reactions to the personal
problems of his co-workers. He considered these as important as those
pertaining to the country's independence, regretting only that he had
not reached the Hindu ideal, as outlined in the Gita, of detachment from

emotions. Gandhi used this enforced rest for introspection and decided to give up his practice of walking with his hands on the shoulders of young girls. In "A Renunciation," an article he wrote for his newspaper during this time, he traced the history of this particular practice, reiterated the purity of his paternal intentions towards the girls involved, acknowledged that he was not unaware of the dangers of the liberty he was taking, and based his renunciation on the grounds of setting a good example to the younger generation.[36]

What is more significant is that in the very first article he was allowed to write by his doctors, Gandhi, meditating on the causes of his ill-health, comes back to the question of his celibacy. He mentions an encounter with a woman during the period of convalescence in Bombay, which not only disturbed him greatly but made him despise himself. In a letter to Prema Kantak, a disciple and confidante in his Sabarmati *ashram*, he elaborates on this incident further.

I have always had the shedding of semen in dreams. In South Africa the interval between two ejaculations may have been in years. I do not remember it fully. Here the time difference is in months. I have mentioned these ejaculations in a couple of my articles. If my *brahmacharya* had been without this shedding of semen then I would have been able to present many more things to the world. But someone who from the age of fifteen to thirty has enjoyed sexuality (*vishya–bhog*)—even if it was only with his wife—whether such a man can conserve his semen after becoming a *brahmachari* seems impossible to me. Someone whose power of storing the semen has been weakened daily for fifteen years cannot hope to regain this power all at once. That is why I regard myself as an incomplete *brahmachari*. But where there are no trees, there are thorn bushes. This shortcoming of mine is known to the world.

The experience which tortured me in Bombay was strange and painful. All my ejaculations have taken place in dreams; they did not trouble me. But Bombay's experience was in the waking state. I did not have any inclination to fulfil that desire. My body was under control. But in spite of my trying, the sense organ remained awake. This experience was new and unbecoming. I have narrated its cause.* After removing this cause the wakefulness of the sense organ subsided, that is, it subsided in the waking

* By remaining inactive and eating well, passions are born in the body.

state.

In spite of my shortcoming, one thing has been easily possible for me, namely that thousands of women have remained safe with me. There were many occasions in my life when certain women, in spite of their sexual desire, were saved or rather I was saved by God. I acknowledge it one hundred percent that this was God's doing. That is why I take no pride in it. I pray daily to God that such a situation should last till the end of my life.

To reach the level of Shukadeva is my goal.* I have not been able to achieve it. Otherwise in spite of the generation of semen I would be impotent and the shedding will become impossible.

The thoughts I have expressed recently about *brahma- charya* are not new. This does not mean that the ideal will be reached by the whole world or even by thousands of men and women in my lifetime. It may take thousands of years, but *brahmacharya* is true, attainable and must be realized.

Man has still to go a long way. His character is still that of a beast. Only the form is human. It seems that violence, is all around us. In spite of this, just as there is no doubt about truth and nonviolence similarly there is no doubt about *brahmacharya.*

Those who keep on burning despite their efforts are not trying hard enough. Nurturing passion in their minds they only want that no shedding of semen take place and avoid women. The second chapter of *Gita* applies to such people.

What I am doing at the moment is purification of thought. Modern thought regards *brahmacharya* as wrong conduct. Using artificial methods of birth control it wants to satisfy sexual passion. My soul rebels against this. Sexual desire will remain in the world, but the world's honor depends on *brahmacharya* and will continue to do so.[37]

Further self-mortification was one of his responses to what he regarded as an unforgivable "lapse." Even the ascetic regimen of the *ashram* now seemed luxurious. Leaving Kasturbai to look after its

---

* Son of Vyasa, Shukadeva is the mythical reciter of the *Bhagavatapurana.* In spite of having married and lived the life of a householder (like Gandhi, he was the father of four sons), in later life he succeeded in conquering his senses to an extent that he rose up to the Heavens and shone there like a second sun.

inmates, he went off to live in a one–room hut in a remote and poverty-stricken, untouchable village. Though he wished to be alone—a wish that for a man in his position was impossible of fulfillment—he soon became the focus of a new community.

Another dark period covers the last two years of Gandhi's life. The scene is India on the eve of independence in 1947. A Muslim Pakistan is soon to be carved out of the country, much against Gandhi's wishes. His dream of Hindus and Muslims living amicably in a single unified state seems to be shattered beyond hope. Gandhi would even postpone independence if the partition of the country could be averted, but his voice does not resonate quite so powerfully in the councils where the transfer of power is being negotiated. The air hangs heavy with clouds of looming violence. Hindus and Muslims warily eye each other as potential murderers . . . or eventual victims. The killings have already started in the crowded back–alleys of Calcutta and in the verdant expanses of rural Bengal, where the seventy–eight–year–old Mahatma is wearily trudging from one village to another, trying to stem the rushing tide of arson, rape, and murder that will soon engulf many other parts of the country. The few close associates who accompany him on this mission of peace are a witness to his despair and helpless listeners to the anguished cries of "*Kya Karun, Kya Karun*?" (What should I do? What should I do?) heard from his room in the middle of the night.[38] "I find myself in the midst of exaggeration and falsity," he writes, "I am unable to discover the truth. There is terrible mutual distrust. Oldest friendships have snapped. Truth and *Ahimsa* (nonviolence) by which I swear and which have to my knowledge sustained me for sixty years, seem to fail to show the attributes I ascribed to them."[39]

For an explanation of his "failures" and sense of despair, Gandhi would characteristically probe for shortcomings in his abstinence, seeking to determine whether the god of desire had perhaps triumphed in some obscure recess of his mind, depriving him of his powers. Thus in the midst of human devastation and political uncertainty, Gandhi wrote a series of five articles on celibacy in his weekly newspaper, puzzling his readers who, as his temporary personal secretary, N. K. Bose, puts it, "did not know why such a series suddenly appeared in the midst of intensely political articles."[40]

But more striking than this public evidence of his preoccupation were his private experiments wherein the aged Mahatma pathetically sought to reassure himself of the strength of his celibacy. These experiments have shocked many and have come to be known as "having naked young women sleep with him when he was old," although their intent and outcome were far removed from the familiar connotations of that suggestive phrase. In the more or less public sleeping arrangements of his entourage while it rested in a village for the night, Gandhi would ask one or another of his few close women associates (his nineteen-year-old granddaughter among them) to share his bed and then try to ascertain in the morning whether any trace of sexual feeling had been evoked, either in himself or in his companion.[41] In spite of criticism by some of his close co-workers, Gandhi defended these experiments, denying the accusation that they could have ill effects on the women involved. Instead, he viewed them as an integral part of the *Yagna* he was performing—the Hindu sacrifice to the gods—whose only purpose was a restoration of personal psychic potency that would help him to regain control over political events and men, a control which seemed to be so fatally slipping away. Again he exploits his desires (and, admittedly, women) for the sake of his cause—the prideful vice of an uncompromisingly virtuous man.

Two Women

In his middle and later years, a number of young women, attracted by Gandhi's public image as the Mahatma, his cause, or his fame, sought his proximity and eventually shared his *ashram* life. These women, who in many cases had left their well–appointed middle- and upper-class homes to take upon themselves the rigors of an ascetic lifestyle, were all else but conventional. Some of them were not only "highstrung" but can fairly be described as suffering from emotional crises of considerable magnitude. Like their counterparts today who seek out well–known gurus, these women too were looking for the therapist in Gandhi as much as the Mahatma or the leader embodying Indian national aspirations. If toning down the intensity of a crippling emotional disturbance and awakening latent productive and creative powers that neither the individual nor the community "knows" he or she possesses is the mark of a good therapist then, as we shall see later, Gandhi was an exceptional one. From women who were a little more than emotional wrecks, he fashioned energetic leaders directing major institutions engaged in the task of social innovation and actively participating in the country's Independence movement.

Gandhi's relationships with these women are fascinating in many ways. First, one is struck by the trouble he took in maintaining a relationship once he had admitted the woman to a degree of intimacy. Irrespective of his public commitments or the course of political events, he was punctilious in writing (and expecting) regular weekly letters to each one of his chosen women followers when they were separated during his frequent visits to other parts of the country or his lengthy spells of imprisonment. Cumulatively, these letters build up a portrait of the Mahatma which reveals his innermost struggles, particularly during the periods of heightened emotional vulnerability, and the role played therein by Woman, as embodied in the collectivity of his chosen female followers.

At their best, the letters are intensely human, full of wisdom about life and purpose. Even at times of stress, they are invariably caring as Gandhi encourages the women's questions, advises them on their intimate problems, and cheerfully dispenses his favorite dietary prescriptions for every kind of ailment. As he writes to one of them: "Your diagnosis is a correct one. The pleasure I get out of solving the *ashram*'s problems, and within the *ashram* those of the sisters, is much greater than that of resolving India's dilemmas."[42]

The second striking characteristic of these letters is what appears to be Gandhi's unwitting effort simultaneously to increase the intimacy with the correspondent and to withdraw if the woman wished for a nearness that crossed the invisible line he had drawn for both of them. The woman's consequent hurt or withdrawal is never allowed to reach a point of breakdown in the relationship. Gandhi employed his considerable charm and powers of persuasion to draw her close again, the hapless woman oscillating around a point between intimacy and estrangement, nearness and distance. The emotions aroused, not only in the women (who were also in close contact with each other) but to some degree in Gandhi, simmered in the hothouse *ashram* atmosphere to produce frequent explosions. In accordance with our narrative intent, let us look at the stories of two of these women, making of them brief tales rather than the novel each one of them richly deserves.

Prema Kantak belonged to a middle-class family from a small town in Maharashtra. She was still a schoolgirl when she heard about Gandhi and the wonderful work he had done for the cause of Indians in South Africa. An only daughter among five sons, she was a favorite of her father and enjoyed more than the usual freedom for a girl of her class and times.

As Prema grew into youth, she was gripped by the fervor of nationalist politics and agonized over personal spiritual questions, interests which Gandhi too combined in his person. Had he not maintained that "politics without religion is dangerous?"

Her first encounter with the great man took place when Gandhi came to address students of her college at Poona. After the talk, she remembers going up to the platform where he was sitting so as to touch his feet in the traditional Indian gesture of respect. Since Gandhi was sitting cross-legged, his feet were tucked under his body. Prema reports:

> Without any mental reservations I touched his knee with my finger and saluted him. With a start he turned to look at me, reciprocated the greetings and looked away. If he but knew that by touching him my heart had blossomed forth with incomparable pride! With that pure touch an electric current ran through my body and I walked home lost in a world of bliss![43]

Sensitive and emotional, intelligent and idealistic, Prema refused to follow the traditional life plan of an Indian girl and get married, perhaps also because of a problematic (most analysts would say "classically hysterical") attitude toward sexuality. "Once, when I was sixteen, I was reading the Bhagavata," she writes, "When I came to the conversation between Kapila and Devahuti,* I learnt how babies come into world. I remember that my hair stood up on the end. I visualised my own conception and was seized with disgust toward my parents and my body! My life seemed dirty! This disgust remained with me for many years."[44] After a bitter quarrel between the daughter and her beloved father, Prema left home to live in a women's hostel. She earned her livelihood by tutoring children while she continued her studies toward a Master's degree.

Prema's fascination for Gandhi and her decision to go and live with him in the *ashram* is quite understandable. In the very nature of the *ashram* life and its ideals, there is a promised protection from disgusting sexuality. In her wishful imagination Gandhi looms up as the ideal parent who will soothe the hurt caused by the disappointment in the real–life one. He is also the admired mentor for Prema's political and spiritual interests, who is capable of comprehending the deeper needs of her soul.

At the age of twenty–three, then, bubbling with innocent enthusiasm,

---

* Kapila is the legendary expounder of the Samkhya system of Hindu philosophy. Devahuti is Kapila's mother.

Prema found herself in Ahmedabad in the Mahatma's presence. As was his wont, at first Gandhi discouraged her. He described to her in detail the hard physical work, the chores of cutting vegetables, grinding grain, cooking meals, cleaning utensils and toilets which awaited her if she adopted the *ashram* life. Prema, exultant in her youthful vitality and idealism, dismissed his cautions as trifles. "I want to do something tremendous!", she exclaimed on one of her very first nights in the *ashram*. With wry humor, Gandhi tried to temper her exuberance without crushing her spirit. "The only tremendous thing you can do just now is go to sleep," he said.[45]

At the start of her stay, when Gandhi was out of town for a few days, Prema had the following dream. She is a little girl reclining in Gandhi's lap. From his breast, a stream of sweet, good milk is flowing straight into her mouth. Prema is drinking the milk and the Mahatma is saying, "Drink, drink, drink more." Prema is replete but the milk continues to flow and Gandhi keeps insisting that she drink more. Prema's clothes and body are thoroughly soaked in milk but the stream is unending. She wakes up in alarm.[46]

On narrating her dream to Gandhi and asking for an interpretation, Gandhi replied, "Dreams can have the quality of purity (*sattvik*) or of passion (*rajasik*). Your dream is a pure one. It means that you feel protected with me."[47] From the orthodox Freudian view, the interpretation cannot be faulted. An instinctive psychoanalyst, Gandhi provides reassurance to the patient and encourages her to give him her trust at this stage of their relationship. Unwittingly following the technical rule of proceeding from the surface to the depths, his interpretation could have been as easily made by an analyst who, for the time being, would have kept his hypotheses on the deeper imports of the dream images—of the symbolic equivalence of milk and semen, Prema's greedy voraciousness, her possible fantasy regarding the persecuting breast, and so on—quietly to himself.

In the *ashram*, the competition among women for Gandhi's attention was as fierce as it is in any guru's establishment today. When he went for his evening constitutional, Gandhi would walk with his hands around the shoulders of the *ashram* girls. There was intense jealousy among them as each kept a hawk's eye for any undue favoritism—the number of times a girl was singled out for the mark of this favor, the duration of time a girl had Bapu's hands on her shoulder and so on. At first Prema felt aggrieved when other girls teased her, "Prema–*ben*, Bapuji does not put his hands on *your* shoulders!" "Why should he? I am not like you to push myself forward!" Prema would reply spiritedly.

"No, he never will. The *ashram* rule is that he can keep his hands only on the shoulders of girls who are younger than sixteen."[48]

Prema felt her deprivation acutely and approached Gandhi who asked her to get the *ashram* superintendent's permission if she wanted him to treat her like the younger girls. Prema's pride was hurt and she responded angrily, "Why should I hanker after your hand so much that I have to go and get permission?" and stalked off. One night, however, Gandhi had gone to the toilet since he was suffering from diarrhoea because of one of his food experiments. He had fainted from weakness and Prema, who had heard him fall, reached his side. Gandhi walked back leaning his body against hers for support and she even lifted him onto the bed. From that night onwards she often accompanied him on his evening walk, with his hand on her shoulder, while she, I imagine, looked around her with the pride of the chosen one, a victor in the secret struggle among the women. In her elation at being closer to him, she tells us, she once kissed his hands saying, "The hand that has shaken the British throne is resting on my shoulders! What a matter of pride!" Gandhi had laughed, "Yes, how proud we all are!" and, clowning, he threw out his chest and strutted about in imitation of a stage emperor.[49]

In 1933, when she was twenty-seven years old, Gandhi begged Prema to give him as *bhiksha* (meritorious alms) a life-long vow of celibacy. Prema wrote back that there was no difficulty in her compliance with his wish as celibacy was in any case her ideal. In unreflected arrogance she added, "I may sleep with any man on the same bed during the whole night and get up in the morning as innocent as a child." Touched on a sore spot, Gandhi reprimanded her on a pride unbecoming a celibate. From mythology he gave examples of those whose pride in their celibacy had gone before a grievous fall. She was no goddess (*devi*), he said, since she still had her periods. For Gandhi believed that in a really celibate woman menstruation stopped completely, the monthly period being but a stigmata of *vikara*, of the sexual distortions of a woman's soul.[50]

Gradually, Prema was trusted with greater and greater responsibilities in running the *ashram*, though her constant struggle, like those of most other women, was for an intimate closeness with Gandhi. He would try to turn her thoughts toward the *ashram* community, instruct her to regard herself as belonging to the community and vice versa. "You are dear to me, that is why 'your' *ashram* is dear to me. Love wants an anchor, love needs touch. It is human nature that not only the mind needs an anchor but also the body and the sense organs," she would argue back.[51] He would ask her to sublimate her emotions, affectionately call her hysterical, explaining that by hysterical he meant someone under an excessive sway of emotions. He would berate her for her lapses and then coax and cajole her back if she showed any signs of withdrawal. Prema felt that the "Old Beloved," her affectionate name for him, had ensnared her. Gandhi replied,

> I do not want to snare anyone in my net. If everyone
> becomes a puppet of mine then what will happen to me? I
> regard such efforts as worthless. But even if I try to trap
> someone you shouldn't lose your self-confidence. Your
> letters prove that you are on guard. Yes, it is true that you
> have always been fearful of being caught in my net. That is
> a bad sign. If you have decided (to throw in your lot with
> me) then why the fear? Or perhaps it is possible that we
> mean different things by the word "ensnare"?[52]

Feeling trapped—by the frustration of her own unconscious wishes in relation to Gandhi, the analyst would say—Prema sought to detach herself from him. She fought with him on what in retrospect seem minor issues. Remaining a devoted follower of Gandhi and his ideals, she was aware of a degree of estrangement from the Mahatma. Prema finally went back to Maharashtra in 1939 and set up an *ashram* in a small village. It was devoted to the fulfillment of Gandhi's social agenda—uplift of the poor and the untouchables, education of women, increasing the self–sufficiency of the village community, and so on. Like the portentous dream after their initial meeting, the separation too is the occasion for a significant dream. In this dream Prema is alone on a vast plain which meets the sky at the horizon. She is sitting in a chair in the middle of this plain with green grass all around her. Behind the chair, she senses the presence of a man. She cannot see him but has no doubt that the man is her protector and her companion. Suddenly four to five beautiful, well–dressed boys come running up to her with bouquets of flowers in their hands. She begins to talk to the boys. More and more children now appear with bouquets. From the sky, flowers begin to rain down upon her. She wakes up with a start. After waking up, when she thinks of the dream, she is convinced that the man standing behind her is Gandhi and that his blessings will always remain with her.[53]

As I reflect on the dream and its context, I cannot help musing (which is less an interpretation of the dream than my associations to it) that perhaps the dream fulfills some of Prema's contradictory wishes. Once again restored to the center of her world with Gandhi, from which she has been recently excluded, she is the celibate *devi* of Hindu mythology on whom gods shower flowers from heaven as a sign of their approbation and homage. On the other hand, she has also become the life–companion of the Mahatma, bearing him not only the four sons Kasturbai had borne but many, many more adoring and adorable children.

Since it was the man rather than what he stood for who was the focus of her emotional life, Prema gradually drifted back to her earlier spiritual interests after Gandhi's death. As she consorted with yogis and mystics, the memory of the Mahatma and the years she had spent with him would become locked up in a corner of her mind, to be occasionally opened and savored privately, a secret solace in times of distress.

In many ways, Madeline Slade was one of the more unusual members of Gandhi's female entourage. Daughter of an admiral in the British Navy who had been a commander of the East Indies Squadron, she was a part of the British ruling establishment, which both despised and feared Gandhi as an implacable foe. Brought up in the freedom of an upper–class English home of the era, Madeline had been dissatisfied and unhappy for years, and tells us that everything had been dark and futile till she discovered Gandhi and left for India when she was in her early thirties.[54] A great admirer of Beethoven—she had thought of devoting her life to the study of his life and music—her plans underwent a drastic change after she read Romain Rolland's book on Gandhi (*Mahatma Gandhi*, 1924). Not wishing to act hastily, she first prepared herself for the ordeal of *ashram* life in India. Madeline went about this task with her usual single–minded determination. She learned spinning and sitting cross–legged on the floor; she became a teetotaler and a vegetarian and learned Urdu. She then wrote to Gandhi expressing her wish and received a cordial reply inviting her to join him.

A tall, strapping woman, handsome rather than pretty, Madeline took avidly to the ascetic part of the *ashram* life. She clung to Gandhi with a ferocity which he found very unsettling, perhaps also because of the feelings which her strong need for his physical proximity in turn aroused ·in him. During the twenty–four years of their association, Gandhi would repeatedly send her away to live and work in other *ashrams* in distant parts of the country. She would have nervous breakdowns as a consequence of these separations and "struggles of the heart" (as she called them) or "spiritual agony" (as Gandhi put it), impetuously rush back to wherever Gandhi was only to be again banished from his presence. He tried to redirect her from her single–minded concentration on him as a person to the cause they both served.

> The parting today was sad, because I saw that I pained you.
> I want you to be a perfect woman. I want you to shed all
> angularities. . . .
>   Do throw off the nervousness. You must not cling to me
> as in this body. The spirit without the body is ever with
> you. And that is more than the feeble embodied imprisoned
> spirit with all the limitations that flesh is heir to. The spirit
> without the flesh is perfect, and that is all we need. This can
> be felt only when we practise detachment. This you must
> now try to achieve.
>   This is how I should grow if I were you. But you should
> grow along your own lines. You will, therefore, reject all I
> have said in this, that does not appeal to your heart or your
> head. You must retain your individuality at all cost. Resist
> me when you must. For I may judge you wrongly in spite
> of all my love for you. I do not want you to impute infalli-
> bility to me.[55]

Madeline, now appropriately renamed Mira by Gandhi after the sixteenth century Indian woman-saint whose infatuation with Krishna was not much greater than Madeline's own yearning for the Mahatma, was however a battlefield of forces stronger than those amenable to reason. She was like the women described by the psychoanalyst Ralph Greenson, who come to analysis not to seek insight but to enjoy the physical proximity of the analyst.[56] Such patients relate a history of achievement and an adequate social life but an unsatisfactory love life characterized by wishes for incorporation, possession, and fusion. Gandhi's attitude to Mira, like that of the analyst with the patient, combined sympathetic listening with the frustration of wishes for gratification—a certain recipe, the mandrake root, for intensifying and unearthing ever more fresh capacities for love in her.[57] It further enhanced what analysts would call her transference to the Mahatma, a type of intense love felt for people who fulfill a role in our lives equivalent to the one fulfilled by parents in our childhood.

The presumption that their relationship was not quite one–sided and that Mira too evoked complex "counter–transference" reactions in

Gandhi is amply supported by his letters to her. Once, in 1927, when Mira had rushed to Gandhi's side on hearing that he was under severe strain, and had promptly been sent back, Gandhi wrote to her:

> I could not restrain myself from sending you a love message on reaching here. I felt very sad after letting you go. I have been very severe with you, but I could not do otherwise. I had to perform an operation and I steadied myself for it. Now let us hope all would go on smoothly, and that all the weakness is gone.[58]

The letter was followed the next day with a post card: "This is merely to tell you I can't dismiss you from my mind. Every surgeon has a soothing ointment after a severe operation. This is my ointment. . ."[59] Two days later, yet another letter followed:

> I have never been so anxious as this time to hear from you, for I sent you away too quickly after a serious operation. You haunted me in my sleep last night and were reported by friends to whom you had been sent, to be delirious, but without any danger. They said, "You need not be anxious. We are doing all that is humanly possible." And with this I woke up troubled in mind and prayed that you may be free from all harm. . .[60]

From prison, where he was safe from her importunate physicality, Gandhi could express his feelings for her more freely. While translating a book of Indian hymns into English for her, he wrote: "In translating the hymns for you I am giving myself much joy. Have I not expressed my love, often in storms than in gentle soothing showers of affection? The memory of these storms adds to the pleasure of this exclusive translation for you."[61] As with his other women, Gandhi could not let Mira get away further than the distance he unconsciously held to be the optimal for his own feelings of well–being.

Like the child on his first explorations of the world who does not venture further from the mother than the length of an invisible string with which he seems attached to her, Gandhi too would become anxious at any break that threatened to become permanent and would seek to draw the woman closer to him.

Chi. Mira,
You are on the brain. I look about me, and miss you. I open
the *charkha* (spinning wheel) and miss you. So on and so
forth. But what is the use? You have done the right thing.
You have left your home, your people and all that people
prize most, not to serve me personally but to serve the
cause I stand for. All the time you were squandering your
love on me personally, I felt guilty of misappropriation.
And I exploded on the slightest pretext. Now that you are
not with me, my anger turns itself upon me for having
given you all those terrible scoldings. But I was on a bed of
hot ashes all the while I was accepting your service. You
will truly serve me by joyously serving the cause. Cheer,
cheer, no more of idle.

To this, Mira added the commentary, "The struggle was terrible. I
too was on a bed of hot ashes because I could feel that Bapu was. This
was one of the occasions when, somehow or other, I managed to tear
myself away."[62]

In 1936, when Gandhi was recovering from his breakdown and had
decided to leave Sabarmati to go and live by himself in a remote village,
Mira thought she finally had a chance to fulfill her deepest longing, to
live with Bapu in the countryside. Gandhi, however, was adamant. He
would stay in the village Mira lived in only if she herself shifted to a
neighboring one. "This nearly broke my heart, but somehow I managed
to carry on, and when Bapu finally decided to come and live in
Seagaon," she writes, "I buried my sorrow in the joy of preparing for
him his cottage and cowshed. For myself I built a little cottage a mile
away on the ridge of Varoda village, and within a week of Bapu's
coming to live in Seagaon I departed for the hut on the hill where I lived
alone with my little horse as my companion."[63] Even this relative
nearness was not to last long as political events inexorably pulled
Gandhi away on his travels.

In 1948, at the time of Gandhi's death, Mira was living in her own
ashram near Rishikesh in the foothills of the Himalayas, devoting
herself to the care of cattle in the nearby villages. Starting one *ashram*
after another, deeper and deeper into the Himalayas, she was to live in
India till 1958 when she decided to return to Europe, almost thirty–five
years after she had first left home in search of Gandhi. I visited her with
a friend in 1964, in the forests above Baden near Vienna where she now
made her home in an isolated farmhouse with a dog and an old Indian
servant from Rishikesh. Gracious but reserved, she offered us tea and

biscuits and perfunctorily inquired about current events in India. She refused to talk about Gandhi, claiming that he did not interest her any longer. What animated her exclusively and what she enthusiastically talked about was Beethoven whom she saw as the highest manifestation of the human spirit. He had been her first love before she read Romain Rolland's book on Gandhi that was to change her life. Working on a biography of Beethoven and with his music as her dearest companion she had come back to the composer after a thirty-five-year detour with Gandhi. Somewhat disappointed, we left her to her new love. Walking toward our car parked a few hundred yards away from the farmhouse, we saw the servant come running up to us, desperation writ large on his lined face: "Sahib, I don't want to live here. I want to go home. Please take me home." I mumbled our apologies for being unable to help and left him standing on the grassy meadow, peering after us in the mild afternoon sun as we drove away.

To place Gandhi's sexual preoccupations in their cultural context, we should remember that sexuality, whether in the erotic flourishes of Indian art and in the Dionysian rituals of its popular religion, or in the dramatic combat with ascetic longings of Yogis who seek to conquer and transform it into spiritual power, has been a perennial preoccupation of Hindu culture. In this resides the reason, puzzling to many non–Indians, why in spite of the surface resemblances between Jungian concepts and Indian thought, it is Freud rather than Jung who fascinates the Indian mind. Many modern Indian mystics feel compelled, in fact, to discuss Freud's assumptions and conclusions about the vagaries and transfigurations of libido while they pass over Jung's work with benign indifference. Indian spirituality is preeminently a theory of "sublimation."

Indian "mysticism" is typically intended to be an intensely practical affair, concerned with an alchemy of the libido that would convert it from a giver of death to a bestower of immortality. It is the sexual fire that stokes the alchemical transformation wherein the cooking pot is the body and the cooking oil is a distillation from sexual fluids. The strength of this traditional aspiration to sublimate sexuality into spirituality, semen into the elixir Soma, varies in different regions with different castes. Yet though only small sections of Indian society may act on this aspiration, it is a well–known theory subscribed to by most Hindus, including non–literate villagers. In its most popular form, the Hindu theory of sublimation goes something like this.

Physical strength and mental power have their source in *virya*, a word that stands for both sexual energy and semen. *Virya*, in fact, is identical with the essence of maleness. *Virya* can either move downward in sexual intercourse, where it is emitted in its gross physical form as semen, or it can move upward through the spinal chord and into the brain, in its subtle form known as *ojas* . Hindus regard the downward movement of sexual energy and its emission as semen as enervating, a debilitating waste of vitality and essential energy. Of all emotions, it is said, lust throws the physical system into the greatest chaos, with every violent passion destroying millions of red blood cells. Indian metaphysical physiology maintains that food is converted into semen in a thirty–day period by successive transformations (and refinements) through blood, flesh, fat, bone, and marrow till semen is distilled— forty drops of blood producing one drop of semen. Each ejaculation involves a loss of half an ounce of semen, which is equivalent to the vitality produced by the consumption of sixty pounds of food.

In another similar calculation with pedagogic intent, each act of copulation is equivalent to an energy expenditure of twenty–four hours of concentrated mental activity or seventy–two hours of hard physical labour.[64] Gandhi is merely reiterating these popular ideas when he says that

> Once the idea, that the only and grand function of the
> sexual organ is generation, possesses men and women,
> union for any other purpose they will hold as criminal
> waste of the vital fluid, and consequent excitement caused
> to men and women as an equally criminal waste of precious
> energy. It is now easy to understand why the scientists of
> old have put such great value upon the vital fluid and why
> they have insisted upon its strong transmutation into the
> highest form of energy for the benefit of society.[65]

If, on the other hand, semen is retained, converted into *ojas* and moved upwards by the observance of *brahmacharya*, it becomes a source of spiritual life rather than cause of physical decay. Longevity, creativity, physical and mental vitality are enhanced by the conservation of semen; memory, will power, inspiration—scientific and artistic—all derive from the observation of *brahmacharya* . In fact, if unbroken (*akhanda*) *brahmacharya* in thought, word, and deed can be observed for twelve years, the aspirant will obtain *moksha* spontaneously.

These ideas on semen and celibacy, I have emphasized above, are a legacy of Indian culture and are shared, so to speak, by Hindu saints and sinners alike. Indeed, the very first published case history in Indian psychoanalytic literature sounds like a parody of Gandhi.

> The patient is a married young man and is the father of several children. He is of religious bent and his ideal in life is to attain what has been called in Hindu literature *jivanmukti*, i.e., a state of liberation from worldly bondages and a perfect freedom from all sorts of passions whether bodily or mental. The possibility of the existence of such a state and of its attainment is never doubted by the patient as he says he has implicit faith in the Hindu scriptures which assert that the realization of *brahma* or supreme entity, results in such a liberation. (He believes) . . . that the only thing he has to do is to abstain from sex of all sorts and liberation will come to him as a sort of reward. . . . Since one pleasure leads to another it is desirable to shun all pleasures in life lest they should lead to sex. The patient is against forming any attachment whether it be with his wife or children or friends or any inanimate object. He is terribly upset sometimes when he finds that in spite of his ideal of no-attachment and no-sex, lascivious thoughts of the most vulgar nature and uncontrollable feelings of love and attraction arise in his mind. . . . In spite of his deep reverence for Hindu gods and goddesses filthy sexual ideas of an obsessional nature come into his mind when he bows before these images.[66]

The "raising of the seed upwards," then, is a strikingly familiar image in the Indian psycho-philosophical schools of self-realization commonly clumped under the misleading label of "mysticism." As Wendy O' Flaherty remarks: "So pervasive is the concept of semen being raised up to the head that popular versions of the philosophy believe that semen originates there."[67] The concept is even present in the *Kamasutra*, the textbook of eroticism and presumably a subverter of ascetic ideals, where the successful lover is not someone who is overly passionate but one who has controlled, stilled his senses through *brahmacharya* and meditation.[68] Indian mythology, too, is replete with stories in which the gods, threatened by a human being who is progressing toward immortality by accruing immense capacities through celibacy and meditation, send a heavenly nymph to seduce the ascetic (even the trickling down of a single drop of sexual fluid counting as a fatal lapse), and thereby reduce him to the common human, carnal denominator.

Of course, given the horrific imagery of sexuality as cataclysmic depletion, no people can procreate with any sense of joyful abandon unless they develop a good deal of scepticism, if not an open defiance, in relation to the sexual prescriptions and ideals of the "cultural superego." The relief at seeing the ascetic's pretensions humbled by the opulent charms of a heavenly seductress is not only that of the gods but is equally shared by the mortals who listen to the myth or see it enacted in popular dance and folk drama. The ideals of celibacy are then simultaneously subscribed to and scoffed at. Whereas, on the one hand, there are a number of sages in the Indian tradition (Gandhi is only the latest one to join this august assemblage), who are admired for their successful celibacy and the powers it brought them, there are, on the other hand, also innumerable folktales detailing the misadventures of randy ascetics. In the more dignified myths, even the Creator is unable to sustain his chastity and is laid low by carnality.

The heavenly nymph Mohini fell in love with the Lord of creation, Brahma. After gaining the assistance of Kama, the god of love, she went to Brahma and danced before him, revealing her body to him in order to entice him, but Brahma remained without passion. Then Kama struck Brahma with an arrow. Brahma wavered and felt desire, but after a moment he gained control. Brahma said to Mohini, go away, Mother, your efforts are wasted here. I know your intention, and I am not suitable for your work. The scripture says, "Ascetics must avoid all women, especially prostitutes." I am incapable of doing anything that the Vedas consider despicable. You are a sophisticated woman, look for a sophisticated young man, suitable for your work, and there will be virtue in your union. But I am an old man, an ascetic Brahmin; what pleasure can I find in a prostitute? Mohini laughed and said to him, "A man who refuses to make love to a woman who is tortured by desire—he is an eunuch. Whether a man be a householder or ascetic or lover, he must not spurn a woman who approaches him, or he will go to Hell. Come now and make love to me in some private place," and as she said this she pulled at Brahma's garment. Then the sages bowed to Brahma, "How is it that Mohini, the best of celestial prostitutes, is in your presence?" Brahma said, to conceal his scheme, "She danced

and sang for a long time and then when she was tired she
came here like a young girl to her father." But the sages
laughed for they knew the whole secret, and Brahma
laughed too.[69]

The piece of gossip that Gandhi "slept with naked women in his old
age" has therefore resounding echoes in the Indian cultural tradition. It
arouses complex emotions in both the purveyor and the listener, namely
a malicious relief together with an aching disappointment that he may
indeed have done so.

The ultimate if ironic refinement of celibacy is found in the tantric
version, where the aspirant is trained and enjoined to perform the sexual
act itself without desire and the "spilling of the seed," thus divorcing the
sexual impulse from human physiology and any conscious or unconscious mental representation of it. The impulse, it is believed, stirs up
the semen in this ritual (and unbelievably passionless) sexual act and
evokes energetic forces that can be rechanneled upwards. This and
other tantric techniques were familiar to Gandhi, whose own deeply
held religious persuasion, Vaishnavism, was pervaded by many such
tantric notions. On the one hand, as we have seen, Gandhi often sounds
like Chaitanya, the fifteenth-century "father" of North Indian Vaishnavism, who rejected a disciple for paying attention to a woman,
saying: "I can never again look upon the face of an ascetic who
associates with women. The senses are hard to control, and seek to fix
themselves on worldly things. Even the wooden image of a woman has
the power to steal the mind of a sage. . . ."[70] On the other hand, however,
Gandhi in his sexual experiments seems to be following the examples
set by other famous Vaishnavas like Ramananda and Viswanatha.
Ramananda, Chaitanya's follower and companion, used to take two
beautiful young temple prostitutes into a lonely garden where he would
oil their bodies, bathe, and dress them while himself remaining "unaf-
fected."[71] The philosopher Viswanatha, it is said, went to lie with his
young wife at the command of his guru: "He lay with her on the bed, but
Viswanatha was transformed, and he did not touch her, as it had been
his custom to do. He lay with his wife according to the instructions of
his guru. . . . and thus he controlled his senses."[72]

There are germs of truth in the signal importance Indian cultural
tradition attaches to sexuality. The notion, arising from this emphasis,
that sexual urges amount to a creative fire—not only for procreation
but, equally, in self-creation—is indeed compelling. Further, a tradition

that does not reduce sexual love to copulation but seeks to elevate it into a celebration, even a ritual that touches the partners with a sense of the sacred, and where orgasm is experienced as "a symbolic blessing of man by his ancestors and by the nature of things," is certainly sympathetic.[73] My concern here has to do with the concommitant strong anxiety in India surrounding the ideas of the "squandering of the sperm" and "biological self-sacrifice." Such ideas and the fantasies they betray cannot help but heighten an ambivalence toward women that verges on misogyny and phobic avoidance. As for self-realization through renunciation of sexual love, I would tend to side with Thomas Mann when he observes:

> It is undeniable that human dignity realizes itself in the two sexes, male and female; so that when one is neither one nor the other, one stands outside the human pale and whence then can human dignity come? Efforts to sustain it are worthy of respect, for they deal with the spiritual, and thus, let us admit in honor, with the preeminently human. But truth demands the hard confession that thought and the spirit come badly off, in the long run, against nature. How little can the precepts of civilization avail against the dark, deep, silent knowledge of the flesh! How little it lets itself be taken in by the spirit![74]

How would Freud, who in his mid-life also chose to become celibate, have regarded Gandhi's celibacy and its intended efficacy? In general, Freud was understandably skeptical about the possibility that sexual abstinence could help to build energetic men of action, original thinkers, or bold reformers. Yet he also saw such attempts at the sublimation of "genital libido" in relative terms:

> The relationship between the amount of sublimation possible and the amount of sexual activity necessary naturally varies very much from person to person and even from one calling to another. An abstinent artist is hardly conceivable; but an abstinent young *savant* is certainly no rarity. The latter can, by his self-restraint, liberate forces for his studies; while the former probably finds his artistic achievements powerfully stimulated by his sexual experience.[75]

It is quite conceivable that Freud would have conceded the possibility of successful celibacy to a few extraordinary people of genuine originality with a self-abnegating sense of mission or transcendent purpose. In other words, he would have agreed with the Latin dictum that "what is allowed to Jove is forbidden to the ox." The psychoanalytic question is, then, not of sublimation but why Gandhi found phallic desire so offensive that he must, so to speak, tear it out by the very roots.

Some of Gandhi's uneasiness with phallic desire has to do with his feeling that genital love is an accursed and distasteful prerogative of the father. In his autobiography, in spite of expressing many admirable filial sentiments, Gandhi suspects his father of being "oversexed" since he married for the fourth time when he was over forty and Putlibai, Gandhi's mother, was only eighteen. In his fantasy, we would suggest, Gandhi saw his young mother as the innocent victim of a powerful old male's lust to which the child could only be an anguished and helpless spectator, unable to save the beloved caretaker from the violation of her person and the violence done to her body. In later life, Gandhi would embrace the cause wherein the marriage of old men with young girls was adamantly opposed with great zeal. He wrote articles with such titles as "Marriage of Old and Young or Debauchery?" and exhorted his correspondents who reported such incidents to fight this practice. The older men he respected and took as his models were those who shared his revulsion with genital sexuality. These were the men who (like Tolstoy and Raichandra) had sought to transform sexual passion into a more universal religious quest or (like Ruskin) into a moral and aesthetic fervor.

If phallic desire was the violent and tumultuous "way of the fathers," genital abstinence, its surrender, provided the tranquil, peaceful path back to the mother. Here Gandhi was not unlike St. Augustine, who too inwardly beheld celibacy garbed in soothing, maternal imagery:

> . . . . there appeared unto me the chaste dignity of Continence, serene, yet not relaxedly gay, honestly alluring me to come and doubt not; and stretching forth to receive and embrace me, her holy hands full of multitudes of good examples; there were so many young men and maidens here, a multitude of youth and every age, grave widows and aged virgins; and Continence herself in all, not barren, but a fruitful mother of children of joys. . . .[76]

More specifically, the psychobiographical evidence we have re-
viewed above is compelling that Gandhi's relationships with women
are dominated by the unconscious fantasy of maintaining an idealized
relationship with the maternal body. This wished for oneness with the
mother is suffused with nurturance and gratitude, mutual adoration and
affirmation, without a trace of desire which divides and bifurcates.
Replete with wishes for fusion and elimination of differences and
limits, Gandhi "perceived" sexual desire, *both* of the mother and the
child, as the single biggest obstacle to the preservation of this illusion.
Many of his attitudes, beliefs, and actions with regard to women can
then be understood as defensive maneuvers against the possibility of
this perception rising to surface awareness.

Since the mother is a woman, a first step in the defensive operations
is to believe that women are not, or only minimally, sexual beings. "I
do not believe that woman is prey to sexual desire to the same extent as
man. It is easier for her than for man to exercise self-restraint,"[77] is an
opinion often repeated in his writings. Reflecting on his own experiences with Kasturbai, he asserts that "There was never want of restraint
on the part of my wife. Very often she would show restraint, but she
rarely resisted me, although she showed disinclination very often."[78]
Whereas he associates male sexuality with unheeding, lustful violence,
female sexuality, where it exists, is a passive, suffering acceptance of
the male onslaught. This, we must again remember, is only at the
conscious level. Unconsciously, his perception of masculine violence
and feminine passivity seem to be reversed, as evident in the imagery
of the descriptions of his few erotic encounters with women. In his very
first adolescent confrontation, he is struck "dumb and blind," while the
woman is confident and aggressive; in England, he is trembling like a
frightened wild animal who has just escaped the (woman) hunter.

The solution to the root problem between the sexes is then, not a
removal of the social and legal inequalities suffered by women—
though Gandhi was an enthusiastic champion of women's rights—but
a thoroughgoing desexualization of the male-female relationship, in
which women must take the lead. "If they will only learn to say 'no' to
their husbands when they approach them carnally. . . . If a wife says to
her husband: 'No, I do not want it,' he will make no trouble. But she has
not been taught. . . . I want women to learn the primary right of
resistance."[79]

Besides desexing the woman, another step in the denial of her desire
is her idealization (especially of the Indian woman) as nearer to a purer
divine state and thus an object of worship and adoration. That is why a

woman does not need to renounce the world in the last stage of life to contemplate God, as is prescribed for the man in the ideal Hindu life cycle. "She sees Him always. She has no need of any other school to prepare her for Heaven than marriage to a man and care of her children."[80] Woman is also

> the incarnation of *Ahimsa. Ahimsa* means infinite love, which, again means infinite capacity for suffering. Who but woman, the mother of man shows this capacity in the largest measure? Let her transfer that love to the whole of humanity, let her forget she ever was, or can be, the object of man's lust. And she will occupy her proud position by the side of the man as his mother, maker and silent leader.[81]

Primarily seeing the mother in the woman and idealizing motherhood is yet another way of denying feminine eroticism. When Millie Polak, a female associate in the Phoenix *ashram* in South Africa, questioned his idealization of motherhood, saying that being a mother does not make a woman wise, Gandhi extolled mother-love as one of the finest aspects of love in human life. His imagery of motherhood is of infants suckling on breasts with inexhaustible supplies of milk. For example, in a letter explaining why the *Gita*, the sacred book of the Hindus, is called Mother, he rhapsodizes,

> It has been likened to the sacred cow, the giver of all desires (sic!). Hence Mother. Well, that immortal Mother gives all the milk we need for spiritual sustenance, if we would but approach her as babies seeking and sucking it from her. She is capable of yielding milk to her millions of babies from her exhaustless udder.
> In doing the Harijan (untouchable) work in the midst of calumny, misrepresentations and apparent disappointments, her lap comforts me and keeps me from falling into the Slough of Despond.[82]

Whereas desexualizing, idealizing, and perceiving only the "milky" mother in the woman is one part of his defensive bulwark which helped in preserving the illusion of unity with the maternal body intact, the other part consists of efforts at renouncing the gift of sexual desire, abjuring his own masculinity. Here we must note that the Hindu

Vaishnava culture, in which Gandhi grew up and in which he remained deeply rooted, not only provides a sanction for man's feminine strivings, but raises these strivings to the level of a religious-spiritual quest. In devotional Vaishnavism, Lord Krishna alone is the male and all devotees, irrespective of their sex, are female. Gandhi's statement that he had mentally become a woman or that he envied women and that there is as much reason for a man to wish that he was born a woman, as for women to do otherwise, thus struck many responsive chords in his audience.

If Gandhi had had his way, there would be no art or poetry celebrating woman's beauty.

> I am told that our literature is full of even an exaggerated
> apotheosis of women. Let me say that it is an altogether
> wrong apotheosis. Let me place one simple fact before you.
> In what light do you think of them when you proceed to
> write about them? I suggest that before you put your pens
> to paper think of women as your own mother, and I assure
> you the chastest literature will flow from your pens, even
> like the beautiful rain from heaven which waters the thirsty
> earth below. Remember that a woman was your mother,
> before a woman became your wife.[83]

Although Gandhi's wished-for feminization was defensive in origin, we cannot deny the development of its adaptive aspects. Others, most notably Erik Erikson, have commented upon Gandhi's more or less conscious explorations of the maternal stance and feminine perspective in his actions.[84] In spite of a welter of public demands on his time, we know of the motherly care he could extend to the personal lives of his followers, and the anxious concern he displayed about their health and well-being, including solicitous inquiries about the state of their daily bowel movements.[85] We also know of the widening of these maternal-feminine ways—teasing, testing, taking suffering upon oneself, and so on—in the formulation of his political style and as elements of his campaigns of militant nonviolence.

We have seen that for Gandhi, the cherished oneness with the maternal-feminine could not always be maintained and was often threatened by the intrusion of phallic desire. His obsession with food at these times, evident in the letters and writings, not only represented a preparation for erecting physiological barriers against desire, but also the strengthening of his psychological defenses, and thus a reinforcement of his spiritual armamentarium. In other words, in his preoccupation with food (and elimination), in his persistent investment of edible physical substances with psychological qualities, Gandhi plays out the "basic oral fantasy," as described by the psychoanalyst Donald Winnicott—"when hungry I think of food, when I eat I think of taking food in. I think of what I like to keep inside and I think of what I want to be rid of and I think of getting rid of it"—whose underlying theme is of union with the mother. His experiments with various kinds of food and a reduction in its intake—in his later years, he abjured milk completely so as not to eroticize his viscera—appear as part of an involuted and intuitive effort to recover and maintain his merger with his mother.

Gandhi's relationship with women and the passions they aroused are, then, more complex than what he reveals in his own impassioned confession. Nor does a recourse to traditional Hindu explanations and prescriptions for their "diagnosis and cure" reflect adequately the depths of the inner life in which his desires found their wellsprings. Beset by conflicts couched in moral terms familiar to Christian and classical psychoanalyst alike, he struggled with the yearnings aroused by the goddess of longing besides the passions provoked by the god of desire. Or, to use a well-known Indian metaphor in which a woman is said to have two breasts, one for her child, another for her husband, Gandhi's unconscious effort to shift from the one breast to the other—from man to child—was not always successful. He was a man in spite of himself. We know that the sensuality derived from the deeply felt oneness with a maternal world, a sensuality that challenges death, energized Gandhi's person, impelled his transcendent endeavors, and advanced him on the road to a freedom of spirit from which India, as well as the world, has profited. Yet we have seen that throughout his life, there were profound periods of emotional turmoil when this original and ultimately illusory connection broke down, emptying him of all inner "goodness" and "power."

7

Masculine/Feminine:
A View from the Couch

On 11 April 1929, Girindrasekhar Bose, the founder and first president of the Indian Psychoanalytical Society, wrote to Freud on the difference he had observed in the psychoanalytic treatment of Indian and Western patients:

> Of course I do not expect that you would accept offhand my reading of the Oedipus situation. I·do not deny the importance of the castration threat in European cases; my argument is that the threat owes its efficiency to its connection with the wish to be female [Freud in a previous letter had gently chided Bose with understating the efficiency of the castration threat.] The real struggle lies between the desire to be a male and its opposite, the desire to be a female. I have already referred to the fact that the castration threat is very common in Indian society but my Indian patients do not exhibit castration symptoms to such a marked degree as my European cases. The desire to be a female is more easily unearthed in Indian male patients than in European. . . . The Oedipus mother is very often a combined parental image and this is a fact of great importance. I have reason to believe that much of the motivation of the maternal deity is traceable to this source.

Freud's reply is courteous and diplomatic:

> I am fully impressed by the difference in the castration

reaction between Indian and European patients and promise to keep my attention fixed on the opposite wish you accentuate. The latter is too important for a hasty decision.[1]

In another paper, Bose elaborates on his observations and explains them through his theory of opposite wishes:

During my analysis of Indian patients I have never come across a case of castration complex in the form in which it has been described by European observers. This fact would seem to indicate that the castration idea develops as a result of environmental conditions acting on some more primitive trend in the subject. The difference in social environment of Indians and Europeans is responsible for the difference in modes of expression in the two cases. It has been usually proposed that threats of castration in early childhood days, owing to some misdemeanour is directly responsible for the complex, but histories of Indian patients seem to disprove this.[2]

Bose then goes on to say that though the castration threat is extremely common—in girls it takes the form of chastisement by snakes—the difference in Indian reactions to it are due to children growing up naked till the ages of nine to ten years (girls till seven) so that the difference between the sexes never comes as a surprise. The castration idea, which comes up symbolically in dreams as decapitation, a cut on a finger, or a sore in some part of the body, has behind it the "primitive" idea of being a woman.

Indeed, reading early Indian case histories, one is struck by the fluidity of the patients' cross-sexual and generational identifications. In the Indian patient, the fantasy of taking on the sexual attributes of both the parents seems to have a relatively easier access to awareness. Bose, for instance, in one of his vignettes tells us of a middle-aged lawyer who, with reference to his parents, sometimes

took up an active male sexual role, treating both of them as females in his unconscious and sometimes a female attitude, especially towards the father, craving for a child from him. In the male role, sometimes he identified himself with his father and felt a sexual craving for the mother; on

the other occasions his unconscious mind built up a composite of both the parents toward which male sexual needs
were directed; it is in this attitude that he made his father
give birth to a child like a woman in his dream.[3]

Another young Bengali, whenever he thought of a particular man,
felt with a hallucinatory intensity that his penis and testes vanished
altogether and were replaced by female genitalia. While defecating he
felt he heard the peremptory voice of his guru asking, "Have you given
me a child yet?" In many of his dreams, he was a man whereas his father
and brothers had become women. During intercourse with his wife he
tied a handkerchief over his eyes as it gave him the feeling of being a
veiled bride while he fantasized his own penis as that of his father and
his wife's vagina as that of his mother.[4]

In my own work, fifty years after Bose's contributions of which till
recently I was only vaguely aware, I am struck by the comparable
patterns in Indian mental life that we observed independently of each
other, and this in spite of our different emotional predilections, analytic
styles, theoretical preoccupations, geographical locations, and historical situations. Such a convergence further strengthens my belief, shared
by every practicing analyst, that there is no absolute arbitrariness in our
representation of the inner world. There is unquestionably something
that resists, a something which can only be characterized by the
attribute "psychical reality," which both the analyst and the analysand
help discover and give meaning to.

It is the ubiquity and multiformity of the "primitive idea of being a
woman" and the embeddedness of this fantasy in the maternal configurations of the family and the culture in India, which I would like to
discuss in my own observations. My main argument is that the "hegemonic narrative" of Hindu culture as far as male development is
concerned, is neither that of Freud's Oedipus nor of Christianity's
Adam. One of the more dominant narratives of this culture is that of
Devi, the great goddess, especially in her manifold expressions as
mother in the inner world of the Hindu son. In India, at least, a primary
task of psychoanalysis, the science of imagination or even (in Wallace
Stevens's words) "the science of illusion" (can one call it *May-
alogy?*)[5]—is to grapple with *Mahamaya*—"The Great Illusion"—as
the goddess is also called. Of course, it is not my intention to deny or
underestimate the importance of the powerful mother in Western
psychoanalysis. All I seek to suggest is that certain forms of the
maternal-feminine may be more central in Indian myths and psyche

than in their Western counterparts. I would then like to begin my exposition with the first fifteen minutes of an analytic session.

The patient is a twenty-six-year-old social worker who has been in analysis for three years. He comes four times a week, with each session lasting fifty minutes and conducted in the classical manner with the patient lying on the couch and the analyst sitting in a chair behind him. He entered analysis not because of any pressing personal problems, but because he thought it would help him professionally. In this particular session, he begins with a fantasy he had while he was in a bus. The fantasy was of a tribe, living in the jungle, which unclothes its dead and hangs them on the trees. M., the patient, visualized a beautiful woman hanging on one of the trees. He imagined himself coming at night and having intercourse with the woman. Other members of the tribe are eating parts of the hanging corpses. The fantasy is immediately followed by the recollection of an incident from the previous evening. M. was visiting his parents' home, where he had lived till recently before he married and set up his own household. This move was not only personally painful but also unusual for his social milieu, where sons normally brought their wives to live in their parental home. An older cousin, with her three-year-old son, was also visiting at the same time. M. felt irritated by the anxious attention his mother and grandmother gave the boy. The grandmother kept on telling the child not to go and play out of the house, to be careful of venturing too far, and so on. On my remarking that perhaps he recognized himself in the nephew, M. exclaimed with rare resentment, "Yes, all the women (his mother, grandmother, his father's brother's wife, and his father's unmarried sister who lived with them) were always doing the same with me."

Beginning with these fifteen minutes of a session, I would like to unroll M.'s conflicts around maternal representations and weave them together with the central maternal configurations of Indian culture. Because of this particular objective, my presentation of further material from M.'s analysis is bound to be subject to what Donald Spence has called "narrative smoothing."[6] A case history though it purports to be a story that is true is actually always at the intersection of fact and fable. Its tale quality, though, arises less from the commissions in imagination than from omissions in reality.

Born in a lower-middle-class family in a large village near Delhi, M. is the eldest of three brothers and two sisters. His memories of growing up, till well into youth, are pervaded by the maternal phalanx of the four women. Like his mother, who in his earliest memories stands out as a distinct figure from a maternal-feminine continuum, to be then reabsorbed in it, M. too often emerges from and retreats into femininity. In the transference, the fantasies of being a woman are not especially disturbing; neither are the fantasies of being an infant suckling at a breast which he has grown onto my exaggeratedly hairy chest. One of his earliest recollections is of a woman who used to pull at the penises of the little boys playing out in the street. M. never felt afraid when the woman grabbed at his own penis. In fact, he rather liked it, reassured that he had a penis at all or at least enough of one for the woman to acknowledge its existence.

Bathed, dressed, combed, and caressed by one or the other of the women, M.'s wishes and needs were met before they were even articulated. Food, especially the milk-based Indian sweets, were constantly pressed on him. Even now, on his visits to the family, the first question by one of the women pertains to what he would like to eat. For a long time during the analysis, whenever a particular session was stressful, because of what he considered a lack of maternal empathy in my interventions, M. felt compelled to go to a restaurant in town where he would first gorge himself on sweets, before he returned home.

Besides the omnipresence of women, my most striking impressions of M.'s early memories is their night setting and their primarily tactile quality. Partly, this has to do with the crowded, public living arrangements of the Indian family. Here, even the notions of privacy are absent, not to speak of such luxuries as separate bedrooms for parents and children. Sleeping in the heat with little or no clothes next to one of his caretakers, an arm or a leg thrown across the maternal body, there is one disturbing memory which stands out clearly. This is of M.'s penis erect against the buttocks of his sleeping mother and his reluctance to move away as he struggled against the feelings of shame and embarrassment that she might wake up and notice the forbidden touch. Later, in adolescence, the mothers are replaced by visiting cousins sharing mattresses spread out in a room or on the roof, furtive rubbings of bodies and occasional genital contact while other members of the extended family are in various stages of sleep.

Embedded in this blissful abundance of maternal flesh and promiscuity of touch, however, is a nightmare. Ever since childhood and persisting well into the initial phases of the analysis, M. would often scream in his sleep while a vague, dark shape threatened to envelop him. At these times, only his father's awakening him with the reassurance that everything was all right helped M. compose himself for renewed slumber. The father, a gentle, retiring man, who left early in the morning for work and returned home late at night, was otherwise a dim figure hovering at the outskirts of an animated family life.

In the very first sessions of the analysis, M. talked of a sexual compulsion which he found embarrassing to acknowledge. The compulsion consisted of traveling in a crowded bus and seeking to press close to the hips of any plump, middle-aged woman standing in the aisle. It was vital for his ensuing excitement that the woman have her back to him. If she ever turned to face M., with the knowledge of his desire in her eyes, his erection immediately subsided and he would hurriedly move away with intense feelings of shame. After marriage, too, the edge of his desire was often at its sharpest when his wife slept on her side with her back to him. In mounting excitement, M. would rub against her and want to make love when she was still not quite awake. If, however, the wife gave intimation of becoming an enthusiastic partner in the exercise, M. sometimes ejaculated prematurely or found his erection precipitately shrivel.

It is evident from these brief fragments of M.'s case history that his desire is closely connected with some of the most inert parts of woman's body, her hips and buttocks. In other words, the desire needs the woman to be sexually dead for its fulfillment. The genesis of the fantasy of the hanging corpse with whom M. has intercourse at night has at its root the fear of the mother's sexuality as well as the anger at their restraint of his explorations of the world. My choice of M.'s case, though, is not dictated by the interest it may hold from a psychoanalytical perspective. The choice, instead, has to do with its central theme, namely the various paths in imagination which M. traverses, in the face of many obstacles, to maintain an idealized relationship with the maternal body. This theme and the fantasized solutions to the disorders in the mother-son relationship are repeated again and again in Indian case and life histories. Bose's observation on the Indian male patient's "primitive idea of being a woman" is then only a special proposition of a more general theorem. The wish to be a woman is one particular solution to the discord that threatens the breaking up of the son's fantasized connection to the mother, a solution whose access to awareness is facilitated by the culture's views on sexual differentiation and the permeability of gender boundaries. Thus, for instance, when Gandhi publicly proclaims that he has mentally become a woman or, quite unaware of Karen Horney and other deviants from the orthodox analytic position of the time, talks of man's envy of the woman's procreative capacities, saying "There is as much reason for a man to wish that he was born a woman as for woman to do otherwise," he is sure of a sympathetic and receptive audience.[7]

In the Indian context, this particular theme can be explored in individual stories as well as in the cultural narratives we call myths, both of which are more closely interwoven in Indian culture than is the case in the modern West. In an apparent reversal of a Western pattern, traditional myths in India are less a source of intellectual and aesthetic satisfaction for the mythologist than of emotional recognition for others, more moving for the patient than for the analyst. Myths in India are not part of a bygone era. They are not "*retained* fragments from the infantile psychic life of the race," as Karl Abraham called them.[8] nor "*vestiges* of the infantile fantasies of whole nations, secular dreams of youthful humanity" in Freud's words.[9]

Vibrantly alive, their symbolic power intact, Indian myths constitute a cultural idiom that aids the individual in the construction and integration of his inner world. Parallel to patterns of infant care and to the structure and values of family relationships, popular and well-known myths are isomorphic with the central psychological constellations of the culture and are constantly renewed and validated by the nature of subjective experience.[10] Given the availability of the mythological idiom, it is almost as easy to mythologize a psychoanalysis, such as that of M., as to analyse a myth; almost as convenient to elaborate on intrapsychic conflict in a mythological mode as in a case historical narrative mode.

Earlier, I advanced the thesis that myths of Devi, the great goddess, constitute a "hegemonic narrative" of Hindu culture. Of the hundreds of myths on her various manifestations, my special interest here is in the goddess as mother, and especially the mother of the sons, Ganesha and Skanda. But before proceeding to connect M.'s tale to the larger cultural story, let me note that I have ignored the various versions of these myths in traditional texts and modern folklore—an undertaking which is rightly the preserve of mythologists and folklorists—and instead picked on their best-known, popular versions.

The popularity of Ganesha and Skanda as gods—psychologically representing two childhood positions of the Indian son—is certainly undeniable. Ganesha, the remover of obstacles and the god of all beginnings, is perhaps the most adored of the reputed 330 million Hindu gods. Iconically represented as a pot-bellied toddler with an elephant head and one missing tusk, he is proportionately represented as a small child when portrayed in the family group with his mother Parvati and father Shiva. His image, whether carved in stone or drawn up in a colored print, is everywhere: in temples, homes, shops, roadside shrines, calendars. Ganesha's younger brother, Skanda or Kartikkeya, has his own following, especially in South India where he is extremely popular and worshipped under the name of Murugan or Subramanya. In contrast to Ganesha, Skanda is a handsome child, a youth of slender body and heroic exploits who, in analytic parlance, may be said to occupy the phallic position.

Ganesha's myths tell us one part of M.'s inner life while those of Skanda reveal yet another. Ganesha, in many myths, is solely his mother Parvati's creation. Desirous of a child and lacking Shiva's cooperation in the venture, she created him out of the dirt and sweat of her body mixed with unguents. Like M.'s fantasies of his femininity, Ganesha too is not only his mother's boy but contains her very essence. Even when indubitably male like Skanda, M. is immersed in the world of mothers which an Indian extended family creates for the child. Skanda, like M., is the son of more than one mother; his father Shiva's seed, being too powerful, could not be borne by one woman and wandered from womb to womb before Skanda took birth. M.'s ravenous consumption of sweets to restore feelings of well-being has parallels with Ganesha's appetite for *modakas*, the sweet wheat or rice balls which devotees offer to the god in large quantities "knowing" that the god is never satisfied, that his belly empties itself as fast as it is filled.[11]

The lean M., like the fat god, craves sweets as a lifeline to the mother's breast; his hunger for the mother's body, in spite of temporary appeasements, is ultimately doomed to remain unfulfilled. M. is further like Ganesha in that he, too, has emerged from infancy with an ample capacity for vital involvement with others.

In the dramatization of M.'s dilemma in relation to the mother, brought to a head by developmental changes that push the child toward an exploration of the outer world while they also give him increasing intimations of his biological rock-bottom identity as a male, Ganesha and Skanda play the leading roles. In a version common to both South India and Sri Lanka the myth goes as follows:

A mango was floating down the stream and Uma (Parvati) the mother, said that whoever rides around the universe first will get the mango [In other versions, the promise is of *modakas* or wives.] Skanda impulsively got on his golden peacock and went around the universe. But Ganesha, who rode the rat, had more wisdom. He thought: "What could my mother have meant by this?" He then circumambulated his mother, worshipped her and said, "I have gone around

136

my universe." Since Ganesha was right his mother gave him the mango. Skanda was furious when he arrived and demanded the mango. But before he could get it Ganesha bit the mango and broke one of his tusks.[12]

Here Skanda and Ganesha are personifications of the two opposing wishes of the older child at the eve of the Oedipus stage. He is torn between a powerful push for independent and autonomous functioning, and an equally strong pull toward surrender and reimmersion in the enveloping maternal fusion from which he has just emerged. Giving in to the pull of individuation and independence, Skanda becomes liable to one kind of punishment—exile from the mother's bountiful presence, and one kind of reward —the promise of functioning as an adult, virile man. Going back to the mother—and I would view Ganesha's eating of the mango as a return to feeding at the breast, especially since we know that in Tamil Nadu, the analogy between a mango and the breast is a matter of common awareness[13]—has the broken tusk, the loss of potential masculinity, as a consequence. Remaining an infant, Ganesha's reward, on the other hand, will be never to know the pangs of separation from the mother, never to feel the despair at her absence. That Ganesha's lot is considered superior to Skanda's is perhaps an indication of Indian man's cultural preference in the dilemma of separation-individuation. He is at one with his mother in her wish not to have the son separate from her, individuate out of their shared anima.[14]

For M., as we have seen, the Ganesha position is often longed for and sometimes returned to in fantasy. It does not, however, represent an enduring solution to the problem of maintaining phallic desire in face of the overwhelming inner presence of the Great Mother. Enter Skanda. After he killed the demon Taraka, who had been terrorizing the gods, the goddess became quite indulgent toward her son and told him to amuse himself as he pleased. Skanda became wayward, his lust rampant. He made love to the wives of the gods and the gods could not stop him. On their complaining to the goddess, she decided to take the form of whatever woman Skanda was about to seduce. Skanda summoned the wife of one god after another but in each saw his mother and became passionless. Finally, thinking that "the universe is filled with my mother," he decided to remain celibate forever.[15]

M., too, we saw, became "passionless" whenever in the bus the motherly woman he fancied turned to face him. But instead of celibacy he tried to hold on to desire by killing the sexual part of the mother, deadening the lower portion of her trunk, which threatened him with impotence. Furthermore, the imagined sexual overpoweringness of the mother, in the face of which the child feels hopelessly inadequate, with fears of being engulfed and swallowed by her dark depths, is not experienced by M. in the form of clear-cut fantasies, but in a recurrent nightmare from which he wakes up screaming.

Elsewhere, I have traced in detail the passage of the powerful, sexual mother through Hindu myths, folk beliefs, proverbs, symptoms, and the ritual worship of the goddess in her terrible and fierce forms.[16] Here, I shall only narrate one of the better-known myths of Devi, widely reproduced in her iconic representations in sculpture and painting, in order to convey through the myth's language of the concrete, of image and symbol, some of the quality of the child's awe and terror of this particular maternal image.

The demon Mahisasura had conquered all the three worlds. Falling in love with the goddess, he sent a message to make his desire known to her. Devi replied that she would accept as her husband only someone who defeated her in battle. Mahisasura entered the battlefield with a vast army and a huge quantity of equipment. Devi came alone, mounted on her lion. The gods were surprised to see her without even armor, riding naked to the combat. Dismounting, Devi started dancing and cutting off the heads of millions and millions of demons with her sword to the rhythm of her movement. Mahisasura, facing death, tried to run away by becoming an elephant. Devi cut off his trunk. The elephant became a buffalo and against its thick hide Devi's sword and spear were of no avail. Angered, Devi jumped on the buffalo's back and rode it to exhaustion. When the buffalo demon's power of resistance had collapsed, Devi plunged her spear into its ear and Mahisasura fell dead.

The myth is stark enough in its immediacy and needs no further gloss on the omnipotence and sexual energy of the goddess, expressed in the imagery of her dancing and riding naked, exhausting even the most powerful male to abject submission and ultimately death, decapitating (i.e., castrating) millions of "bad boys" with demonic desires, and so on. The only feature of the myth I would like to highlight, and which is absent both in M.'s case vignette and in the myths narrated so far, is that of the sword- and spear-wielding Devi as the phallic mother. In the Indian context, this fantasy seems more related to Chasseguet-Smirgel's notion of the phallic mother's being a denial of the adult vagina and the feelings of inadequacy it invokes rather than allowing its traditional interpretation as a denial of castration anxiety.[17] In addition, I would see the image of the goddess as man–woman (or, for that matter, of Shiva as *ardhanarishwara*, half man-half woman), as incorporating the boy's wish to become a man without having to separate and sexually differentiate from the mother, to take on male sexual attributes while not letting go of the feminine ones.

The myth continues that when Devi's frenzied dancing did not come to an end even after the killing of the buffalo demon, the gods became alarmed and asked Shiva for help. Shiva lay down on his back and when the goddess stepped on her husband she hung out her tongue in shame and stopped. Like M.'s gentle and somewhat withdrawn father, who was the only one who could help in dissipating the impact of the nightmare, Shiva too enters the scene supine, yet as a container for the great mother's energy and power. In other words, the father may be unassuming and remote, yet powerful. First experienced as an ally and a protector (or even as a covictim), the father emerges as a rival only later. The rivalry, too, in popular Indian myths and most of my case histories, is less that of Oedipus, the power of whose myth derives from the son's guilt over a fantasized and eventually unconscious parricide. The Indian context stresses more the father's envy of what belongs to the son—including the mother—and thus the son's persecution anxiety as a primary motivation in the father-son relationship. It is thus charged with the fear of filicide and with the son's castration, by self or the father, as a solution to the father-son competition. Shiva's beheading of Ganesha, who on the express wish of his mother stood guard at her private chambers while she bathed, and the replacement of his head by that of an elephant, the legends of Bhishma and Puru, who renounced sexual functioning in order to keep the affections of their father intact, are some of the better-known illustrations.[18] But the fate of fathers and sons and families and daughters are different narratives; stories yet to be told, texts still to be written.

Cultural ideas and ideals of masculinity and femininity, then, manifested in their narrative form as myths, pervade the innermost experience of the self. One cannot therefore speak of an "earlier" or "deeper" layer of the self beyond cultural reach. As a "depth psychology," psychoanalysis dives deep, but in the same waters in which the cultural river too flows. Preeminently operating from within the heart of the Western myth, enclosed in the *mahamaya* of Europe—from myths of ancient Greece to the "illusions" of the Enlightenment—psychoanalysis has had little opportunity to observe from within, and with empathy, the deeper import of other cultures' myths in the workings of the self.

The questions relating to the "how" of this process are bound up with the larger issue of the relationship between the inner and outer worlds, which has been of perennial psychological and philosophical interest. It is certainly not my intention to discuss these questions at any length. I would only like to point out that apart from some notable exceptions, such as Erik Erikson, who both held aloft and significantly contributed to the vision of a "psychoanalysis sophisticated enough to include the environment,"[19] most theorists generally underestimated the impact of culture on the development of a sense of identity—the construction of the self, in modern parlance. Freud's "timetable" of culture, entering the psychic structure relatively late in life as the "ideology of the superego," has continued to be followed by other almanac makers of the psyche.[20]

Even Heinz Kohut, as Janis Long has shown, does not quite follow the logical implications of his concept of "selfobject."[21] These are, of course, the aspects of the other which are incorporated in the self and are experienced as part of one's own subjectivity. Kohut, too, follows Freud in talking of a "culture selfobject" of later life, derived in part from cultural ideals, which helps in maintaining the integrity and vitality of the individual self.[22] Yet the idea of selfobject which goes beyond the notion of a budding self's relatedness to the environment, to the environment's gradual transmutation into *becoming* the self, implies that "*what* the parents respond to in a developing child, *how* they respond and what they present as idealizable from the earliest age"[23]—surely much of it a cultural matter—will be the raw material for the child's inner construction of the self, including the gender self.

In other words, a caretaker's *knowing* of the child, a knowing in which affect and cognition are ideally fused, is in large part cultural and forms the basis of the child's own knowing of him- or herself. The notion that the construction and experience of the self is greatly influenced by culture from the very beginning does not imply that there is no difference between individual faces and cultural masks, no boundary between inner and outer worlds. The tension between the two is what gives psychoanalysis and literature much of their narrative power. All I seek to emphasize here is that this boundary cannot be fixed either in time or psychic space. It is dynamic, mobile, and constantly subject to change.

8

An Ending

This book has presented the viewpoints of the actors involved in the drama of the sexes in India. Each chapter was, so to speak, a site report, an account of intimate relations as perceived and defined by the participants. For a long time, the ruling orthodoxy in social sciences devalued such personal testimony as "subjective." It preferred to see individual feelings, desires, and fears as an epiphenomena of macro forces located in genes, culture, history, social or sexual division of labor. Conflicts between the sexes could then be attributed to one of the many theories in vogue: "programmed genetic traits," "system of patriarchy," "mode of production," and so on.[1]

The intent of this study has been to avoid conceptualizing Indian gender relations in such abstract terms and to eschew the overobjectification of human behavior that this kind of theorizing entails. Instead, I have tried to highlight the personal and the "storied" nature of relations between the sexes. I have then interpreted these stories in a way which circumvents the second common weakness of most social theories—their lack of appreciation of the role of sexuality and the irrational in human affairs.

As portrayed in various narratives, from films to folktales, from autobiographies to case histories, gender relations seem impelled more by hostility than tenderness or love. The fantasies entertained by each sex in relation to the other are pervaded as much by hatred and fear as by desire and longing. Partly, this has to do with the very nature of the narrative enterprise. It is difficult to conceive of a tale which will hold our attention and grip our imagination if it is totally devoid of conflict between its sexual protagonists. Somewhere along the course of the story, men and women must misunderstand, mistrust, or hurt each other, even if the chasm that opens up between them is temporary and will be ultimately spanned. Stories in which lovers continue to dwell in a blissful paradise with nary a serpent to intrude upon the stillness of their repose, dramas that show couples in complete harmony undisturbed by the slightest tremor, are understandably rare.

Apart from the needs of the narrative form, our cultural conditioning makes us unwilling to accept the existence of a fundamental hostility between the sexes. For its own reproduction, each society has to focus on the positive aspects of this most basic of all human relationships. Official spokesmen of a culture, the apologists and sentimentalists of its tradition, must necessarily hold up affirmative models. In India, for instance, the images of the *pativrata* wife and the couple that is like the *ardhanarishwara*, have been held up as the immanent reality of the relations between the sexes. Hostility and rage will tend to be dismissed as pathological episodes, avoidable occurrences which are neither an integral part of the sexual drama nor inherent in the man-woman connection.

Yet we know from psychoanalysis that sexual desire which compels men and women toward each other in promised fulfillment of a timeless yearning has another darker face. In desire, the body's wanting and its violence, the mind's yearning for sexual pleasure but also the need to rid itself of ancient pain and noxious hate, the excitement of orgasm and the fierce exultation of possession, all flow together.[2] Forces of selfishness, destruction, and ambivalence always accompany the quest for sexual pleasure and spiritual union. In the coming together of the sexes, we resent the violation of the body's boundaries even while we want nothing more than to transcend them. We fear sexuality's threat to the tenuous order we have carved out for ourselves during the course of our development—even as we long for its dissolution into a veritable *mahabhava*, a "great feeling" that will allow us ecstasy and exaltation rather than the small joys and dribbles of pleasure we extract from our inner order.

Little wonder, then, that theories of gender relations, especially as they pertain to the oppression of women, founder on the ambiguities and ambivalences of sexuality. Although oppressed in many societies, women still cannot be likened to any other exploited group, such as the blacks in South Africa or the "untouchable" castes in India. Blacks and whites, low and high castes do not have to deal with the conscious and unconscious exigencies of a mutual desire which is both a promise of self-enhancement, even transcendence, and a threat of disintegration to the self. Nor do they, or any other pairing of the oppressor and the oppressed, need each other—in Plato's comment on his myth of the origin of sexes—for "reuniting our original nature, making one of two, healing the state of man."[3]

Coming back to Indian gender relations, we saw that in plumbing the fantasies of men and women we reached a common bedrock in human imagination. Here, the similarities in the ways the sexes perceive each other—within the culture and between cultures—seem to outweigh differences, at least as far as patriarchal societies are concerned. This universality springs from our infantile discovery, struggling against wishes and fears which would have it otherwise, that we are either one sex or the other—as are our beloved and hated caretakers and siblings. In other words, the universally shared features in the portrayed amalgamation of fact, fantasy, and folklore men call "woman" and women "man", spring from a common psychical reality and are relatively independent of my looking at these portraits from an "essentialist" psychoanalytic perspective.

Universality is not synonymous with uniformity. Within global clusters of human longings and anxieties, cultures can and do accentuate certain elements more than others. In India, too, the dominant Hindu culture has created its own brand of sexual mythology through the fantasies it has chosen to underscore in its narratives. Thus, for instance, it is generally true that the public discourse of all patriarchal societies stresses motherhood as the primary if not the sole reason of woman's existence whereas, ironically, it underplays the importance of fatherhood for a man. Hindus, too, share this widespread orientation wherein the image of woman as mother is sought to be superimposed upon and thereby to obliterate the picture of woman as a sexual being. Yet during the superimposition, and this is the most salient feature of male fantasy in India, what emerges is a composite image of the *sexual mother*. As we saw, she is an overwhelming presence in the men's preception of woman, a being to whom one is in danger of ceding both genitals and the self. She pervades Gandhi's agonizings but also looms large in clinical case histories, myths, and in popular narratives.

Following on the sexual mother's heels, her features somewhat more amorphous and blurred, is the unfaithful mother. We saw her appear prominently in the story of the snake woman, although her visage is also glimpsed in other narratives as well as in proverbs and pronouncements of ancient law-givers. In her willing or "unwilling" sexual submission to the "father," she is the universal betrayer of a boy's first love and primordial passion. A favorite heroine of psychoanalytic stories for over eight decades, there is nothing more one can say about her and she need not detain us further here.

The dread of the sexual mother and the rage at the unfaithful one are dealt with in our stories in certain specific ways. In other words, the culture highlights some defenses more than others. Whereas viewing women as dangerous antagonists to be subdued through violence or denying their existence altogether in a misogynous turn to the world of men are responses common enough across patriarchies, Indian fantasy seems to favor one particular defensive mode. This is desexualization, either of the self or of the woman. In the former, a renunciation of the awareness of sexual differentiation is sought in ascetic longings or in the quiescence of the infant at the breast. In the latter, the woman is unsexed, à la Hindi movies, by turning her into a maternal automaton, a dispenser of emotional pap, or into an androgynous virgin.

Similarly, the women in the universe of our stories share many characteristics of their counterparts in other patriarchal societies. We see the same private protest, at every level of society, against a socialization which has emphasized the mother and housewife as the woman's primary gender roles. As in the marriage scenes from North Indian novels, there is a constant struggle, waged through the bickerings of household life, for a redressal of the uneven balance of power between the sexes. In the sexual metaphors availed of by fantasy, the woman would wrest the phallus—the symbol of male power—or have one of her own in the male child she therefore craves and subsequently invests with the full might of her emotions.

Yet what strikes me most in the Indian woman's fantasy, as reflected in the narratives, is less a burning rage than an aching disappointment. Her imagination seems propelled by the longing for a single two-person universe—which the women from the slums called a *jodi*—where the affirmation of her female body and the recognition of her feminine soul take place simultaneously. The longing is for an idealized phallus which will serve as a "transitional object" in the consolidation of her feminine identity. To elaborate upon what was earlier mentioned only in passing, I would speculate that this yearning has its roots in the course taken by the girl's interactions with adult men in the family, especially the father. We know that a girl's sexual awakening depends to a considerable extent upon the seductive attention paid to her by the "father," an entity who, according to the family type, can mean a single individual or the collectivity of paternal men. Within the space demarcated by the incest taboo, the father must make the girl conscious of his masculine appreciation of her femininity, especially at various critical periods of her development, such as early childhood and adolescence.[4] Without this "normal seduction," the daughter's desire may remain relatively inhibited. If, however, after early demonstrations of erotically tinged interest, the father withdraws or otherwise absents himself from the girl's life, she will be deprived of a sustained experience of a more normal father-daughter relationship, which would have helped her gradually to desexualize the father. A sense of rejection of her eroticism and a fixing of her inner state of aroused desire on the paternal phallus of early childhood may then be a few of the consequences which constitute an area of vulnerability in the women's psyche.

What gives this particular developmental sequence in individual women's lives a wider cultural significance is the structure of relationship between the sexes in the family, especially "father" and "daughter," in large sections of Hindu upper castes. After the first four or five years of a child's life, the father progressively (and at puberty, even precipitately) withdraws from interaction with the growing girl, who is taken over and assimilated into the community of women at an early age. Although the entrance into the women's community mitigates the slights and shields the girl from humiliation at the hands of the surrounding patriarchal order, it also has the result of isolating her from the "father." This increases the longing for the idealized paternal phallus which is manifested in various ways, including the menacing movie images of rape by father figures.

Leaving the question of origins aside, the stories make it abundantly clear that in contrast to the fear and dread pervading men's fantasies of women, anger and disappointment are a large part of the women's feelings in relationship to men.

At the end, we will do well to remember that the Indian tale of intimate relations, or for that matter that of any culture, has many renderings. The sober, dark version recounted here, in which the dream of intimacy verges on a nightmare and where the sexual union of man and woman becomes a zone of genital combat, is preeminently a psychoanalytic story. As such it is only one building block in that imposing and mysterious edifice we call love, and which houses our soul in a more essential way than the buildings of straw and mud, bricks and mortar, sheltering our bodies.

Notes

Chapter 1

1. Richard Shweder and N. Much, "Determination of Meaning: Discourse and Moral Socialization" (Committee on Human Development, University of Chicago, 1985, unpublished).

2. Margaret T. Egnor, "The Ideology of Love in a Tamil Family" (Hobart and Smith College, 1986, unpublished).

3. Oliver Sacks, *The Man Who Mistook His Wife for a Hat* (New York: Harper and Row, 1987), 147.

4. Ibid., 148.

5. Robert Goldman, "The Serpent and the Rope on Stage: Popular, Literary, and Philosophical Representations of Reality in Traditional India," *Journal of Indian Philosophy* 14 (1986): 149–69.

6. As the termites say to Brahma in *Devi Bhāgvata*, "Nidrābhangah kathāchedo/Dampatyoh pritibhedanam/Śiśumātrivibhedaśca Brahmātyasamam smrtam" (To disturb one in sleep, to interrupt a story, to separate a husband and wife as also mother and child—these things are tantamount to killing a brahmin). Cited in Vettam Mani, *Puranic Encyclopaedia* (Delhi: Motilal Banarsidas, 1985), 183.

7. John A. Robinson and Linda Hawpe, "Narrative Thinking as Heuristic Process," in *Narrative Psychology: The Storied Nature of Human Conduct*, ed. T. Sarbin (New York: Praeger, 1986), 123.

8. A. MacIntyre, *After Virtue* (Notre Dame, Ind.: University of Notre Dame Press, 1981), 201.

9. See Robert S. Wallerstein, "Psychoanalysis as a Science: A Response to New Challenges," *Pyschoanalytic Quarterly* 55 (1986): 414–51; M. Sherwood, *The Logic of Explanation in Psychoanalysis* (New York: Academic Press, 1968).

10. Donald Spence, "Psychoanalytic Competence," *International Journal of Psychoanalysis* 62, no. 1 (1981): 113–24.

11. For an exceptionally fine summary of the object-relations view, see J.R. Weinberg and S. Mitchell, *Object Relations in Psychoanalytic Theory* (Cambridge: Harvard University Press, 1982).

12. Meredith Anne Skura, *The Literary Use of Psychoanalytic Process*

147

(New Haven: Yale University Press, 1981), 178.

13. For an interesting new approach influenced by Lacan, see Peter Brooks, *Reading for the Plot* (New York: Knopf, 1984).

14. Meredith Anne Skura, *The Literary Use of the Psychoanalytic Process* (New Haven: Yale University Press, 1981).

15. Dale Boesky, "Correspondence with Miss Joyce Carol Oates," *International Review of Psychoanalysis* 2 (1975): 482.

Chapter 2

1. Rajinder Singh Bedi, *Ek Chadar Maili Si* (Allahabad: Neelam Prakashan, 1961).

2. Margaret T. Egnor, "The Ideology of Love in a Tamil Family" (Hobart and Smith College, 1986, unpublished), 112–13.

3. For a collection of Indian proverbs on women, see *Bharatiya Kahawat Sangraha*, vol. 2, ed. V. O. Narvane (Pune: Triven Sangam, 1979), 641–51. The translations of the folksayings in this section are my own.

4. *Rig Veda* 10.145 and 10.159. Ed. F. Max Mueller (London: Oxford University Press, 1890–92).

5. *Rig Veda* 10.18.8.

6. *Ramayana* 3.57.17. Eds. G.H. Bhatt *et. al.* (Baroda: Oriental Institute, 1960–75)

7. My clinical impressions on the actual and potential sexual intimacy of the woman and the younger brother of the husband are supported by the results of at least one empirical study. Behere and Natraj found that the sexual partner of almost half of the men who admitted to premarital relations was the wife of the elder brother. See P. B. Behere and G. S. Natraj, "*Dhat* Syndrome: The Phenomenology of a Culture-bound Syndrome," *Indian Journal of Psychiatry* 26, no. 1 (1984): 76–78.

8. Krishna Sobti, *Mitro Marjani* (New Delhi: Raj Kamal Prakashan, 1967).

9. Sigmund Freud, "A Special Type of Choice of Object Made by Men" (1910), Standard Edition of the Works of Sigmund Freud (London: Hogarth Press, 1952), vol. 2, 163–76. Hereafter referred to as *Standard Edition*.

10. *The Laws Of Manu*, 3.56, ed. F. Max Mueller, trans. G. Buehler (Oxford: Clarendon Press, 1886), 85.

11. Ibid., 9.26, 332.

12. Ibid., 9.3, 328.

13. Ibid., 9.11, 329.

14. Ibid., 9.12.

15. Ibid., 9.14, 330.

16. Ibid., 9.15.

17. Ibid., 9.17.

18. Ibid., 9.20.

19. *Bharatiya Kahawat Sangraha*, vol. 2.

20. *The Laws of Manu*, 3.47.

21. D.W. Winnicott, *The Family and Individual Development* (London:

Tavistock, 1965), 40. The original insight is, of course, by John Stuart Mill in his 1869 essay, "The Subjection of Women."

22. G. Lakoff and M. Johnson, *Metaphors We Live By* (Chicago: University of Chicago Press, 1980).

Chapter 3

1. On the influence of film values on Indian culture, see Satish Bahadur, *The Context of Indian Film Culture* (Poona: National Film Archives of India, n.d.). See also the various contributions in *Indian Popular Cinema: Myth, Meaning, and Metaphor*, special issue of the *India International Quarterly* 8, no. 1 (1980).

2. Robert J. Stoller, *Perversion* (New York: Pantheon Books, 1975), 55.

3. Sudhir Kakar, *The Inner World: A Psychoanalytic Study of Childhood and Society in India* (Delhi: Oxford University Press, 1978), chap.3.

4. Arjun Appadurai and Carol Breckenridge, "Public Culture in Late Twentieth-Century India" (Department of Anthropology, Pittsburgh: University of Pennsylvania, July 1986, unpublished).

5. See Bruno Bettelheim, *The Uses of Enchantment* (New York: Knopf, 1976).

6. Some of these films are *Junglee, Bees Saal Baad, Sangam, Dosti, Upkaar, Pakeeza, Bobby, Aradhana, Johnny Mera Nam, Roti Kapda aur Makan, Deewar, Zanjeer, Sholay, Karz, Muqaddar Ka Sikandar,* and *Ram Teri Ganga Maili.*

7. Wendy O'Flaherty, "The Mythological in Disguise: An Analysis of Karz," in *Indian Popular Cinema*, note 1 above, 23–30.

8. Sudhir Kakar and John M. Ross, *Tales of Love, Sex, and Danger* (London: Unwin Hyman, 1987), chap. 3.

9. *Mahabharata*, 5,144.5–10. The English translation is taken from J.A.B. von Buitenen, ed. and trans.,*The Mahabharata* (Chicago: University of Chicago Press, 1978), 453.

10. The psychological effects of modernization have been discussed in E. James Anthony and C. Chiland, eds., *The Child in His Family: Children and Their Parents in a Changing World* (New York: John Wiley, 1978).

11. Martha Wolfenstein and Nathan Leites, *Movies: A Psychological Study* (Glencoe, Ill.: Free Press, 1950).

12. Joyce McDougall, *Theatres of the Mind* (New York: Basic Books, 1986).

Chapter 4

1. These are the types of tales which come closest to what Lüthi described as "one-dimensional." See Max Lüthi, *European Folktale: Form and Nature* (Philadelphia: Institute for the Study of Human Issues, 1982), 4–10. See also Kamil V. Zvelebil, *Two Tamil Folktales* (Delhi: Motilal Banarsidas, 1987), i–vii, for an exhaustive discussion of the formal characteristics of a similar Tamil narrative. The translations of the stories from *Kissa Tota Myna* are mine.

2. In this sense they are also what Arthur Deikman has called "teaching stories." See Arthur Deikman, *The Observing Self* (Boston: Beacon Press, 1982), 153.

3. Sudhir Kakar, *The Inner World: A Psychoanalytic Study of Childhood and Society in India* (Delhi: Oxford University Press, 1978), 87ff.

4. Robert P. Goldman, "Fathers, Sons, and Gurus: Oedipal Conflict in Sanskrit Epics," *Journal of Indian Philosophy* 8 (1978): 325–92.

5. *Mahabharata Virataparva* 2:14. Translated by P.D. Roy (Calcutta: Oriental Publishing, n.d.).

6. Zvelebil, *Two Tamil Folktales*, 131–36. A.K. Ramanujan has collected a folktale, "The Serpent Lover," from Karnataka, which is identical with the second part of the adventures of Princess Standing Lamp.

7. See David Will, "Psychoanalysis and the New Philosophy of Science," *International Review of Psychoanalysis* 13 (1986): 163–74.

8. See Manfred Lurker, *Adler und Schlange: Tiersymbolik in Glauben und Weltbild der Volker* (Tubingen: 1983) and Balaji Mundkur, *The Cult of the Serpent: An Interdisciplinary Survey of Its Manifestations and Origins* (Albany: State University of New York Press, 1983).

9. For a summary discusssion of Oedipal and pre-Oedipal meanings of the snake symbolism, see Philip Slater, *The Glory of Hera* (Boston: Beacon Press, 1966), 88ff.

10. B. E. F. Beck and Peter J. Claus, eds., *Folktales of India* (Chicago: University of Chicago Press, 1986), 27.

11. Bruno Bettelheim, *The Uses of Enchantment* (New York: Knopf, 1976), 282–310.

12. Stuart Blackburn and A.K. Ramanujan, eds., *Another Harmony: New Essays in the Folklore of India* (Berkeley: University of California Press, 1986), 14.

Chapter 5

1. Oscar Lewis, *La Vida* (New York: Vintage Books, 1968), xlii.

2. B. Bernstein, *Soziale Struktur und Sprachverhalten* (Amsterdam: 1970).

3. *Mahabharata: Anusasana Parva*, translated by P.D. Roy (Calcutta: Oriental Publishing, n.d.), 325.

4. For a discussion of Jungian notions, see R.M. Stein, "Coupling-Uncoupling: Bindung und Freiheit," in *Analytische Psychologie* 14 (1983): 1–14.

5. Heinz Kohut, *The Analysis of the Self* (New York: International Universities Press, 1971).

Chapter 6

1. For psychoanalytic perspectives on autobiography, see Robert Steele, "Deconstructing Histories: Toward a Systematic Criticism of Psychological Narratives," in *Narrative Psychology*, ed. T. R. Sarbin (New York: Praeger, 1986). See also Erik H. Erikson, "In Search of Gandhi: On the Nature of Psychohistorical Evidence," *Daedalus* (Summer 1968).

2. For a discussion of Nabokov's *Speak, Memory*, see Sudhir Kakar and John Ross, *Tales of Love, Sex, and Danger* (London: Unwin Hyman, 1987), chap. 8.

3. M. K. Gandhi, *Satya na Prayoga athva Atma-Katha* (translated by Mahadev Desai as *The Story of My Experiments with Truth*) (Ahmedabad: Navjivan Prakashan Mandir, 1927), 10; henceforth referred to as *Autobiography*.

4. Ibid., 31.

5. V. S. Naipaul, *India: A Wounded Civilization* (New York: Knopf, 1976), 102–6.

6. Gandhi, *Autobiography*, 75.

7. Ibid., 69.

8. A.K. Ramanujan, "Hanchi: A Kannada Cinderella," in *Cinderella: A Folklore Casebook*, ed. A. Dundes (New York: Garland Publishing, 1982), 272.

9. M.K. Gandhi, *Bibi Amtussalam ke nam patra* [*Letters to Bibi Amtussalam*], (Ahmedabad: Navjivan, 1960), 70.

10. Gandhi, *Autobiography*, 91.

11. Ibid., 205.

12. Pyarelal, *Mahatma Gandhi: The First Phase*, (Bombay: Sevak Prakashan), 213.

13. Ibid., 207.

14. M.K. Gandhi, *The Collected Works of Mahatma Gandhi* (Delhi: Publication Division, Government of India, 1958), vol. 3, letters of 30 June 1906 to Chaganlal Gandhi and H.V. Vohra, 352–54; henceforth referred to as *Collected Works*.

15. Ibid., 208–9.

16. Gandhi, *Collected Works*, vol. 5, 56.

17. M. K. Gandhi, *To the Women* (Karachi: Hingorani, 1943), 49–50, 52.

18. Gandhi, *To the Women*, 194.

19. M.K. Gandhi, "Yervada Mandir," in *Selected Works*, vol. 4 (Ahmedabad: Navjivan, 1968), 220.

20. Ibid.

21. M.K. Gandhi, "Hind Swaraj," in *Collected Works*.

22. Millie G. Polak, *Mr. Gandhi: The Man* (Bombay: Vora & Co., 1949), 63–64.

23. Gandhi, "Yervada Mandir," 223.

24. St. Augustine, *The Confessions*, trans. E.R. Pusey (New York: Modern Library, 1949), 227.

25. Ibid., 228.

26. Gandhi, *Autobiography*, 324.

27. Ibid., 210.

28. Ibid., 501.

29. Ibid., 24.

30. St. Augustine, *Confessions*, 162.

31. Gandhi, *Collected Works*, vol. 37 (1928), "Speech on the Birth Centenary of Tolstoy" (10 September 1928), 258.

32. Ibid., 265.

33. Gandhi, *Autobiography*, 209.

34. Gandhi, *Collected Works*, vol. 37 (1928), 258.

35. Gandhi, *Collected Works*, vol. 36 (1927–28), letter to Harjivan Kotak, 378.

36. Gandhi, "Ek Tyag,"in *Harijanbandhu*, 22.9.35.

37. M.K. Gandhi, *Kumari Premaben Kantak ke nam patra* [*Letters to Premaben Kantak*], (Ahmedabad: Navjivan, 1960), 260–62 (my translation).

38. The best eyewitness account of Gandhi's Bengal period is by N.K. Bose, Gandhi's temporary secretary, who was both a respectful follower and a dispassionate observer: see his *My Days with Gandhi* (Calcutta: Nishana, 1953).

39. Ibid., 52.

40. Ibid., 189.

41. In his *Key to Health*, rewritten in 1942 in the middle of another depressive phase following the widespread violence of the "Quit India" movement and the death of his wife in prison, Gandhi had hinted at this kind of self-testing: "Some of my experiments have not reached a stage when they might be placed before the public with advantage. I hope to do so some day if they succeed to my satisfaction. Success might make the attainment of *brahmacharya* comparatively easier." See *Selected Works*, vol. 4, 432. For a compassionate and insightful discussion of these experiments, see also Erik H. Erikson, *Gandhi's Truth* (New York: Norton, 1969), 404.

42. Gandhi, *Kumari Premaben Kantak ke nam patra*, 16.

43. Ibid., 19.

44. Ibid., 188.

45. Ibid.

46. Ibid., 39.

47. Ibid.

48. Ibid.

49. Ibid.

50. Ibid., 190.

51. Ibid., 151.

52. Ibid., 173.

53. Ibid., 369.

54. See Mira Behn, ed., *Bapu's Letters to Mira* (1924–48) (Ahmedabad: Navjivan, 1949) and *The Spirit's Pilgrimage* (London: Longman, 1960).

55. Behn, ed., *Bapu's Letters to Mira*, 27–28.

56. R. Greenson, *The Technique and Practice of Psychoanalysis* (New York: International Universities Press, 1967), 338–41.

57. See Martin S. Bergman, "Transference Love and Love in Real Life," in J. M. Ross, ed., *International Journal of Psychoanalytic Psychotherapy* 11 (1985–86): 27–45.

58. Behn, ed., *Bapu's Letters to Mira*, 42.

59. Ibid.

60. Ibid., 43.

61. Ibid., 71.

62. Ibid., 88.

63. Ibid., 166.

64. For an elaborate description of some of these popular psychological ideas in English, see Swami Sivananda, *Mind: Its Mysteries and Control* (Sivanandanagar: Divine Life Society, 1974), chap. 28, and Swami Narayanananda, *The Mysteries of Man, Mind, and Mind-Functions* (Rishikesh: Universal Yoga Trust, 1965), chap. 19.

65. Gandhi, *To the Women*, 71.

66. G. Bose, "All or None Attitude in Sex," *Samiksa* 1 (1947): 14.

67. Wendy O'Flaherty, *Women, Androgynes, and Other Mythical Beasts* (Chicago: University of Chicago Press, 1980), 45.

68. See Wendy O'Flaherty, *Asceticism and Eroticism in the Mythology of Siva* (London: Oxford University Press, 1973), 55.

69. *Brahmavaivarta Purana*, 4.31, 4.32, 1.20, 4.33, 1.76; English translation abridged from O'Flaherty, *Asceticism and Eroticism in the Mythology of Siva*, 51.

70. Cited in Edward C. Dimock, Jr., *The Place of the Hidden Moon* (Chicago: University of Chicago Press, 1966), 154.

71. Ibid., 54.

72. Ibid., 156.

73. See Ramchandra Gandhi, *Brahmacharya* (Department of Philosophy, University of Hyderabad, 1981, unpublished), 26.

74. Thomas Mann, *Joseph and His Brothers* (London: Secker and Warburg, 1959), 719.

75. Sigmund Freud, "Civilized Sexual Morality and Modern Nervousness" (1908), *Standard Edition*, vol. 9, 197.

76. St. Augustine, *Confessions*, 165.

77. Gandhi, *To the Women*, 81.

78. Ibid., 60.

79. Ibid., 57.

80. Polak, *Mr. Gandhi*, 34.

81. Gandhi, *To the Women*, 28–29.

82. Behn, ed., *Bapu's Letters to Mira*, 141.

83. Gandhi, *To the Women*, 102.

84. Erikson, *Gandhi's Truth*.

85. Ved Mehta, *Mahatma Gandhi and His Apostles* (New Delhi: Indian Book Co., 1977), 13.

86. D.W. Winnicott, "Appetite and Emotional Disorder," in *Collected Papers* (London: Tavistock Publications, 1958), 34.

Chapter 7

1. T.C. Sinha, "Psychoanalysis in India," *Lumbini Park Silver Jubilee Souvenir* (Calcutta: 1966), 66.

2. G. Bose, "The Genesis of Homosexuality," (1926) *Samiksa* 4, no. 2 (1950): 74.

3. G. Bose, "A New Theory of Mental Life," *Samiksa* 2 (1948): 158.

4. G. Bose, "The Genesis and Adjustment of the Oedipus Wish," *Samiksa* 3, no. 1 (1949): 222–40.

5. The coinage is by Clifford Geertz, who used it in the Symposium on Culture and Human Development sponsored by Committee on Human Development, University of Chicago, 5–7 November 1987.

6. Donald P. Spence, "Narrative Smoothing and Clinical Wisdom," in *Narrative Psychology*, ed. T. Sarbin (New York: Praeger, 1986).

7. M.K. Gandhi, *To the Women* (Karachi: Hingorani, 1943), 194 and 28–29. Karen Horney, "The Flight from Womanhood: The Masculinity Complex in Women as Viewed by Men and Women," in *Feminine Psychology* (New York: Norton, 1967).

8. Karl Abraham, *Dreams and Myths: A Study in Race Psychology* (New York: The Journal of Nervous and Mental Health Publishing Company, 1913), 72.

9. Sigmund Freud, "Creative Writers and Daydreaming," in *Standard Edition*, Vol. 9, 152.

10. Gananath Obeyesekere, *Medusa's Hair: A Study in Personal and Cultural Symbols* (Chicago: University of Chicago Press, 1981).

11. Paul B. Courtright, *Ganesha* (New York: Oxford University Press, 1986), 114.

12. G. Obeyesekere, *The Cult of Pattini* (Chicago: University of Chicago Press, 1984), 471.

13. Margaret T. Egnor, *The Ideology of Love in a Tamil Family* (Hobart and Smith College, 1984, unpublished).

14. Sudhir Kakar, "Psychoanalysis and Anthropology: A Renewed Alliance," *Contributions to Indian Sociology* 21, no. 1 (1987), 88.

15. The Sanskrit source of the myth is the *Brahma Purana*, 81. 1–5. For an English translation see Wendy O'Flaherty, *Asceticism and Eroticism in the Mythology of Siva* (London: Oxford University Press, 1973), 204.

16. Sudhir Kakar, *The Inner World: A Psychoanalytic Study of Childhood and Society in India* (Delhi: Oxford University Press, 1978).

17. J. Chasseguet-Smirgel, "Feminine Guilt and the Oedipus Complex," in *Female Sexuality*, ed. J. Chasseguet-Smirgel (Ann Arbor: University of Michigan Press, 1964), 94–134. For traditional views, see Sigmund Freud, "Fetishism," *Standard Edition*, vol. 21 (1924) and "Splitting the Ego in the Process of Defence," *Standard Edition*, vol. 23 (1940). See also R.C. Bak, "The Phallic Woman: The Ubiquitous Fantasy in Perversions," *The Psychoanalytic Study of*

the Child, vol. 23, 15–16.

18. Sudhir Kakar and John Ross, *Tales of Love Sex, and Danger* (London: Unwin Hyman, 1987).

19. Erik H. Erikson, *Childhood and Society* (New York: Norton, 1950).

20. Sigmund Freud, "New Introductory Lectures on Psychoanalysis," *Standard Edition*, vol. 22 (1922).

21. Janis Long, "Culture, Selfobject, and the Cohesive Self," paper presented at the American Psychological Association Meetings, August 1986.

22. Heinz Kohut, *Self Psychology and Humanities*, ed. D. Strozier (New York: Norton, 1985), 224–31.

23. Janis Long, "Culture, Selfobject, and the Cohesive Self," 8.

Chapter 8

1. For an exhaustive discussion of these conceptual models see A. Brittan and M. Maynard, *Sexism, Racism and Oppression*, (Oxford: Basil Blackwell, 1984).

2. Sudhir Kakar and John Ross, *Tales of Love, Sex and Danger* (London: Unwin Hyman, 1987).

3. Plato, "Symposium" in B. Jowett, trans., *The Portable Plato*, (New York: Viking Press, 1950), p. 145.

4. See, for instance, L. H. Tessman, "A Note on the Father's Contribution to the Daughter's Ways of Loving and Working," in S. H Cath *et. al.*, eds., *Father and Child: Developmental and Clinical Perspectives*, (Boston: Little Brown, 1982), 219–38.

Index

Index